Choice

~~WHITE~~ PRIVILEGE

LIBRTY HILL PRESS

Choice ~~WHITE~~ PRIVILEGE

WHAT'S RACE GOT TO DO WITH IT?

an intellectual, biblical
and experiential rebuttal
to critical race theory

MELISSA TATE

Liberty Hill Press
2301 Lucien Way #415
Maitland, FL 32751
407.339.4217
www.libertyhillpublishing.com

Unless otherwise indicated, Scripture quotations taken from the
Holy Bible, New International Version (NIV). Copyright © 1973, 1978,
1984, 2011 by Biblica, Inc.™. Used by permission. All rights reserved.

Scripture quotations taken from the English Standard Version (ESV).
Copyright © 2001 by Crossway, a publishing ministry of Good News
Publishers. Used by permission. All rights reserved.

Scripture quotations taken from the King James Version
(KJV)–*public domain.*

Scripture quotations taken from the New King James Version (NKJV).
Copyright © 1982 by Thomas Nelson, Inc. Used by permission. All
rights reserved.

Printed in the United States of America.

Paperback ISBN-13: 978-1-6628-0074-0
Dust Jacket ISBN-13: 978-1-6628-0075-7
Ebook ISBN-13: 978-1-6628-0076-4

CONTENTS

FOREWORD

Melissa Tate is a fellow African. She was born and raised in Zimbabwe and I was born and raised in South Africa. Both of us, and our families, feel privileged to be able to call America our home.

The nation of America has always been a beacon of liberty to the nations of the world. I do not think that most Americans truly understand how important America's standing in the world is. If Americans fail to maintain their liberties—given by God and guaranteed by the Constitution—then when America falls, the whole world collapses with her!

Like Melissa, I understand the extreme threat to our liberties imposed by both socialism and then communism. The latter which will swiftly take the place of the former, once it is fully established. Throughout history, the enemies of liberty have imposed communism on countries in stages. At every turn, they have employed lies, propaganda, and disinformation to achieve their goals. The way they succeed is by brainwashing the populace.

Critical Race Theory and "White Privilege" is a smokescreen—designed to confuse people, to manipulate them, to create division and strife, and ultimately to collapse the nation.

Unfortunately, many people have believed the propaganda and yet others don't know what to believe. Melissa exposes the hypocrisy and lies surrounding the subject and brings clarity and understanding to current events.

The only way for a country to survive this threat to Liberty is for the people to know the truth. The ultimate Truth is found in the Word of God.

Each and every one of us is created in the image of God. We may have been born in different nations, into different families, and we may have a different skin color, but we each have one thing in common—free will and freedom of choice.

Melissa shows that it is not white privilege, but choices, that determine the direction and quality of our own life.

Each and every one of us—black, white, and brown—can choose to see ourselves through the eyes of God. We can choose to apply His principles to our life. We can recognize that we have the ability to steer the ship of our life to where we want to go. When you realize that you are not a victim and that no one can hold you back— you will accomplish for more than you ever dreamed possible. When you take responsibility for your own life, there are no limits to what you can achieve.

I highly recommend this book and I encourage everyone to read it with an open heart and mind, and to share it with your friends.

Pastor Rodney Howard Brown – September 2020

INTRODUCTION

"WHITE PRIVILEGE." WHAT DOES RACE HAVE TO DO WITH privilege? American society is becoming more racially divided, and every aspect of life is now being filtered through the lens of race. Judging people collectively based solely on the color of their skin is now embraced, not only as normal but as a virtuous practice.

If you're White, you're automatically part of a the "privileged class" of "oppressors," regardless of your own personal circumstances. If you're Black (or any minority) you're automatically an oppressed victim that needs coddling and saving. This is the message being transmitted to us on both a conscious and subconscious level, coming from every sphere of society. In media, entertainment, education, politics, at our jobs, and, sadly, even in our churches.

How did we, as a society, drift so far from the ideals of Martin Luther King Jr., who dreamed of a time when a person would be judged not by the color of their skin but by the content of their character? Evidently, this has not been an organic progression of our society, according to my research. Rather, these are the fruits of a concerted and coordinated effort by progressive left ideologues that have imbedded themselves in American society over many decades.

As an immigrant from Zimbabwe, an African country that fell to socialism, I am cognizant of what it looks like when this sort of ideology begins to take root in a nation. I lived through the economic collapse of my nation, which began with the same racial rhetoric and division I'm witnessing in America today. It was a rhetoric that pitted Black and White Zimbabweans against each other. The ensuing racial conflict sparked the beginning of the collapse of a once-great nation.

Over the last fifty to sixty years, Marxian ideology has crept into American society, virtually undetected, and embedded itself in every sphere of influence under the guise of progress and progressivism. What we are witnessing today is the culmination of an ideology that has been in motion for decades and has only began to rear its ugly head in mainstream culture.

According to David Satter, author and researcher who writes about the Soviet Union, by the end of the twentieth century, Marxism had been responsible for the death of over a hundred million people around the world. Many thought the ideology had been eradicated, but it was not. Due to the increasing unpopularity of the ideology, Marxism was forced to reinvent itself and reconvene to its present, more subtle, stealthier form.

In this book, I take you on a journey of discovery of the who, what, when, why, and how of identity politics in America and how racial division and racism is being used as a political weapon to conquer America from within.

I discuss critical race theory as the operating system of this neo-Marxist plot to overthrow America's founding principles on a macro level. On a micro-level, I discuss how this ideology is used to keep Blacks (and other minorities) in America in a perpetual state of victimhood and grievance. This state of mind has made many susceptible to manipulation, into being political pawns for this agenda. It has also blinded people to the opportunities they have around them in modern day America.

"For as he thinks in his heart, so *is* he" (Prov. 23:7, NKJV). Many in the Black community have had their very existence tied to grievances of the past, bitterness, and unforgiveness that has given rise to a mental state that I believe stifles their progress as individuals and as a society.

Too many Americans have been relegated to a mental prison where they're taught to see themselves as nothing more than "Black in America." And being Black in America, we're told, is a life sentence of oppression by 'the White man', who is out to ensure our destruction as Black people.

Is this true? In this book, that is what I explore, through the eyes of a Black woman who grew up in Africa and immigrated to America. I am Black in America, but my experience in America has been a contradiction to the prevailing narrative that my skin color is supposed to be disadvantageous or an impediment to my success and wellbeing in America.

I came to the United States at the age of nineteen, with nothing but a suitcase full of clothes and a few hundred dollars in my pocket. With hard work and determination, I was able to achieve what I would certainly describe as the American dream. I am just as Black as any other Black person in America, so why has my experience been different? There must be other variables at play besides my skin color. Is it, perhaps, the fact that I have a different mind-set and perspective on life? I believe so.

One observation I made earlier about Black Americans in general, was that the number one characteristic by which they define and identify themselves, is the color of their skin. This is not true of other races and cultures. Most people place other characteristics above skin color and race when they define their identity.

Black American journalist Jason Whitlock wrote a powerful piece shedding light on how White liberal progressives have persuaded Black people in America to elevate their "blackness" above all else—above faith, intelligence, and freedom.

He writes, "I am repulsed by the people who have worked tirelessly for more than 400 years to convince Black people that our skin color is our most prized asset and defining characteristic. It has now led to our mental enslavement." He goes on to say "The root of my disdain is biblical. Sixty years ago, the hallmark of black culture was religious faith. It carried us through slavery, Jim Crow segregation, lynching and was the power source of Dr. Martin Luther King Jr.'s Civil Rights Movement. Over the last 55 years, the stewards of American culture have worked to disconnect black people from our religious faith, our salvation. Black pride is our new religion."

When you are taught from a young age to regard your entire existence through the narrow lens of your race, and then you're told that your race is an impediment, it limits your capacity and potential to be everything you are called to be.

The main defining characteristic I have always identified with is being a child of God. This idea was instilled in me from a young age, growing up as a Christian in Zimbabwe and later accepting Christ as my Lord and Savior. My skin color barely makes the top ten identifying characteristics that drive my life or defines my existence. Living my life through the consciousness of how God sees me is part of the mind-set that has allowed me to dare to live outside the box modern society wants to place me in. Knowing that God says I am an infinite being with limitless potential, created in His image, is what defines me.

So who are these stewards steering this stifling frame of mind, and why is it a necessary stratagem to keep so many minds shackled? In this book, we will explore how the left has worked hard to disconnect Black Americans from their history of strong religious faith and God-centered families. This culture of faith and family has, in many cases, been replaced with a counterfeit culture and religion—the culture and religion of "blackness."

The progressive left has made themselves the arbiters of the hallmarks of blackness. These include speaking Ebonics, dealing drugs, having multiple "baby mamas," and, of course, the highest form of blackness—being a victim of racism. If you speak proper English, value education or do not identify with being a victim, then you're not "authentically Black" and are often accused of "acting White" or being a "sellout." This is according to the progressive stewards of Black culture.

In researching African American history and culture for this book, I discovered the true authentic Black American culture that endured through the atrocities of slavery, built thriving communities during the time window after slavery and before the 1960s. In spite of the systemic oppression that existed in that era, Black people were surpassing Whites in many metrics and indicators of success. This period in history is largely ignored.

In this book, we will discuss how so-called progressive policies and identity politics (largely introduced in the 1960's) are not only destroying the Black community but tearing the fabric of America by design.

By no means do I make the argument in this book that racism doesn't exist. Racism is a sin that has always existed and will always exist. I, therefore, explore racism and racial bias in the book in its multiple dimensions. The question I ask and answer is whether or not racism is systemic and of consequence to one's life today. Racism has never had any significance in my life, not because it doesn't exist but because I have never given it the power to affect my life.

I wrote this book because it broke my heart to see how so many of my fellow Americans are being pigeonholed, manipulated and how their potentials and destinies are being stolen from them. This is all done for a political agenda that I believe will destroy this great country and its people if left unchallenged.

Coming from a once great nation that fell following racial divisions, I've been able to pick up on the warning signs. The events that took place following the tragic death of George Floyd was the tipping point that really prompted me to research this issue of race in America. Prior to this, the topic of race and racism was of very little or no interest to me.

In 2015, during the Republican primary, I became drawn in by the fanfare that surrounded candidate Donald Trump. Even though I've always been a conservative and a supporter of the Republican Party, I increasingly become dissatisfied with the party. It became clear that they were complicit in much of what I disliked about what was going on in Washington, DC, among our elected officials. They almost never seemed to put up a fight against what I saw as an encroachment by the far left. Republicans didn't keep many of their promises to their conservative constituents.

During the first debate, I was immediately drawn to Trump's blunt style and thought he was the wrecking ball we needed to shake things up in corrupt Washington, DC. I joined Twitter only to follow Trump and found myself tweeting and becoming part of a conservative community on the site. In doing so, I gained a large following that climbed to over a half a million. I didn't sign up with the intent of becoming a "social media influencer" or political commentator, but it turned out that way.

Since then, I felt God calling me out of business and into politics. Many doors have opened for me in the realm of politics. I have been connected to many prominent republicans and conservatives in the process. I've even been to the White House twice and have met President Trump. Meeting the president of the United States at the White House is quite an achievement, and I'm proud of it.

When I took an interest to politics, I wanted to focus my political activism on issues that affected the church. My goal has always been to see America preserve its godly founding principles, which make it the greatest nation on the planet. One that has afforded me great opportunity for self-advancement. I wanted to see the American church rallied to engage in the culture war by reclaiming the sphere of influence it once occupied (e.g., politics, education, media, entertainment, business, family) but lost.

As someone to whom God speaks through dreams, I've had many dreams in which I'm speaking to the Black community on issues of race. For a while, I was like Jonah running from Nineveh. I wanted to stay as far away as possible from the topic of race. However, the events of 2020 put a fire in me to speak on this issue, because I now see it is so central to restoring America and its people to their God-given destiny and purpose.

It is my desire to see Americans of every race, color, and creed, united under the banner of just being Americans. America has been a melting pot of people, who were historically united by deep patriotism and allegiance to the nation, its principles and ideals. Historically, people who migrated to America assimilated into the American culture and embraced their new national identity as Americans. Today, America seems to be losing its national and cultural cohesion. The stewards of the zeitgeist, seem to illuminate our differences, while the things that unite us as Americans are disregarded.

I believe Christians and conservatives alike can stop the advances of racial division and Marxism in America. Not only that, we can also reverse the decades-long tide of the progressive leftward slide of American culture and politics. I discuss at length how we can start engaging culture and reclaiming the spheres of influence we once dominated.

CHAPTER 1

PRIVILEGE—THE FALLACY OF WHITE PRIVILEGE

M y first real-life encounter with the concept of White privilege was in 2014. It happened when my first-born son was only three years old and was attending a Montessori school. You see, my husband and I had agreed that we would make the necessary sacrifices to educate our children in a Christian school. Based on location and reputation, we settled on a Catholic Montessori school that was near our home. One day, in our son's second preschool year, we received a notice that the school was going to have a guest speaker. The topic of the schoolwide lecture (for pre-K through eighth grade) was "White privilege." I had never heard this term before. Immediately, it did not sit well with me. Anything that singles out people based on race is always a red flag for me.

After researching what it was, I was mortified. Why would my son's school consider introducing such a topic? A topic that would make young and impressionable children self-conscious about their race?

"So, let me get this straight," I thought. "They're going to teach my three-year-old child that his skin color automatically makes him a victim of oppression? They're going to teach him that his skin color is an impediment to his success/wellbeing and that his

White classmates already have an advantage over him, merely because they have white skin? What?"

The following day, my husband and I scheduled a meeting with the headmaster, who defended the merits of the program. He said it was important for Whites to recognize that they are privileged so that they can do their part to combat racism. I could not believe what I was hearing. To boil it down, the school was going to teach White children to have a superiority complex that they were supposed to feel guilty about. Needless to say, we immediately withdrew our son from the school.

Think about the negative psychological impact it would have had on my son to be told by an authoritative figure, before he's even had the life experience to judge for himself, that he is at a disadvantage among his peers because of the color his skin.

I was not going to expose my son to such a defeatist doctrine, which would teach him to see himself as a victim or as less than his classmates. A sense of victimhood or feeling of inferiority because of my race is not something I've ever internalized. It has never been a part of my experience in life. So why would I let someone teach my son to see himself through the narrow lens of being a victim of oppression?

Victimhood is never a breeding ground for success, in any sphere of life. It's a mind-set that stifles motivation and progress and sets people up for failure. I've always taught my children that, in America, they have the privilege to pursue their dreams. With hard work, good choices, a bit of determination, and persistence, they can and will succeed at life. I teach them that they are the captains of their own ships.

Some of the core values I was raised with in Zimbabwe were personal responsibility and self-determination. These basic values have been the guiding force in my own life and are significant contributing factors to my success.

At the age of nineteen, I arrived in the US to start college in the winter semester. All I had was a suitcase, the clothes on my back—including a borrowed coat—and a few hundred dollars. But after four years of hard-work and determination, I was able to graduate with a bachelor of science in business administration, get a corporate job, and move on to start my own business.

By the time I was twenty-seven, I owned a successful business with five employees and annual gross sales north of a million dollars. Therefore, I reject the concept of privilege as a function of being White. I've had many opportunities and privileges that have brought me to where I am today, including the greatest privilege—the opportunity to come to America to pursue my lifelong dreams.

As a Black person, the term "White privilege" and the narrative that surrounds it is actually very offensive to me. I find it very patronizing. The idea behind it is that my blackness is some sort of disability or impediment. That because I'm Black, I'm somehow limited in what I can do and who I can become. That because I'm Black, I have no privilege of any kind. That only White people can have privilege. That I'm oppressed. That, to function, I need White people to recognize their privilege, bow down with guilt, and apologize for their racism. So, the false narrative goes.

In my opinion, this ideology itself comes from a place of White supremacy. It's a backhanded form of White supremacy. White people who espouse this idea of White privilege seem to see themselves as superior and have a White-savior superiority complex. They can virtue signal in a patronizing way, by "recognizing" their privilege or supremacy over others.

To them, by default, I am automatically classified as a victim who needs saving, and the bar of expectations is subsequently lowered because I can't possibly function without assistance. I have been derided many times by White progressives for daring to proclaim that I'm not a victim. I'm not oppressed. Their response is usually something like, "You must hate your own race." They say this because, according to them, victimology is part of what is supposed to make me "authentically Black." By saying that I'm not oppressed, I'm declaring that I'm their equal, and that makes progressive White saviors very upset, as I have come to observe.

On the other hand, Black people and minorities in agreement with this ideology wear oppression like a badge. They believe they simply don't have the wherewithal to improve their lives, due to forces beyond their control. They've been raised to believe that the societal odds are overwhelmingly against them, so they adopt passivity and victimology rather than striving to better themselves. It's easier to be a victim than it is to take personal responsibility, assess your particular situation, and improve it. It's so much easier to blame outside indicators for one's circumstances, which are sometimes a result of a series of their own bad choices.

FROM ACADEMIA TO MAINSTREAM

Regardless of my own personal feelings and opinions on the concept of White privilege, it's important that people understand that it's just one component of a much larger and deeply troubling philosophy. One that has taken root in Western culture within the framework of an academic philosophy known as critical race theory. We will dive deep into the origins of this concept in chapter 6.

I felt compelled to write this book to dispel this false doctrine. I have witnessed too many well-meaning people (including many well-respected pastors, friends, and family members) fall into the deception of this extremely destructive ideology. Unfortunately, this philosophy has permeated every sphere of society in America. If left unchecked, it will devour this nation from within.

White privilege and its parent philosophy, critical race theory, were primarily discussed in the halls of modern-day academia, in America's universities. Previously, these institutions were places for higher learning, where one could find a free marketplace of ideas to be exchanged. But they have quietly been transformed and reduced to what I call indoctrination camps, where diversity of ideas is no longer tolerated.

As the Iron Curtain of Communism/Marxism crumbled, people often joked that Marxism was dead everywhere—except in American universities. This stereotype is not without merit. According to a panel discussion hosted by American Enterprise Institute, titled "The Close-Minded Campus? The Stifling of Ideas in American Universities," self-identifying Marxists outnumber classical liberals and conservatives. Herbert London, an American academic, suggested that up to ten thousand Marxist professors roamed college campuses. He said this of Marxism in our universities: "Every discipline has been affected by its preachment, and almost every faculty now counts among its members a resident Marxist scholar."

American universities are now, sadly, places where students are no longer taught how to think critically but what to think.

White privilege, along with so many other so-called progressive ideas, has emerged from these dark corners of academia and into the light of the mainstream culture. In 2020, this was especially true. After the tragic death of George Floyd, allegedly at the hands of a White police officer, the issue of race has taken center stage.

DEFINING WHITE PRIVILEGE

In order to properly understand White privilege, it is imperative to understand its origin, and more importantly, it's political objectives.

Privilege, as defined by Merriam-Webster's dictionary is, "a special right, advantage, or immunity granted or available only to a person or group." Based solely on this definition, the notion of White privilege in modern-day America falls apart quickly. White people in America do not systemically possess any special right or advantage. There are no laws in place that grant Whites special privileges in this country in 2020.

Based on the dictionary definition of *privilege*, I would argue that it is Black privilege that exists. America does have numerous laws on the books that give special rights and advantages to Black Americans and other minority groups.

A couple of examples of these privileges include Black student scholarships and Black business owner loans. Plus, affirmative action requires employers to hire African Americans to reach government mandated quotas. Often, hiring decisions are based on reaching these racial quotas, and, as a result, the most qualified candidate may not get hired, solely because they have the wrong skin color. The qualification bar for Black Americans is lawfully lowered. In some cases, this gives Blacks an unfair advantage over other, more qualified individuals of other races. (Ironically, that sounds like systemic racism to me.)

The same is true for affirmative action for college admission. SAT test score requirements are lowered for Black Americans. That means a Black student does not need to score as high as White or Asian students to be accepted at a university. This is what I call the bigotry of low expectations. Why does the bar have to be lowered for Black people? More on that later, but these are just a few systemic advantages or privileges that Black Americans are afforded in America.

So, based on the actual dictionary definition of privilege, the notion of privilege based solely on your skin color being White, collapses.

But of course, it's a common practice of the progressive left to redefine words and attach their own meanings so that the words conform to how they want the conversation framed. Thus, "privilege" and "White privilege" have different and deeper meanings in the context of the left's argument for White privilege.

The definition of White privilege varies, depending on who is defining it or the purposes for which they are using it. The definition can be nebulous and ever evolving at times, so it can be hard to keep up. So for argument's sake, we'll use the most popular and commonly used definition of White privilege by the progressive left. The Anti-Defamation League (ADL) a far-left organization that purports to "fight hate," defines White privilege as follows:

"A term for unearned and often unseen or unrecognized advantages, benefits or rights conferred upon people based on their membership in a dominant group (e.g., White people, heterosexual people, males) beyond what is commonly experienced by members of the marginalized group. Privilege reveals both obvious and less obvious unspoken advantages that people in the dominant group may not recognize they have, which distinguishes it from overt bias or prejudice. These advantages include cultural affirmations of one's own worth, presumed greater social status and the freedom to move, buy, work, play and speak freely."

WHITE PRIVILEGE—ORIGINS AND FALLACY

Peggy McIntosh, a celebrated feminist, is said to be the originator of the White privilege concept. In the late 1980s, she came up with the term "unacknowledged male privilege." She defined this as "the unearned advantages men have in society by mere virtue of being born male." Likewise, she believed there was also White privilege, and so the terminology of White privilege was born.

In 1988, Peggy published the article "White Privilege and Male Privilege: A Personal Account of Coming to See Correspondences through Work in Women's Studies." In this article, Peggy lists forty-six privileges she enjoyed as a White person. She argues not only that being White benefitted her but that her "whiteness oppressed other races and gave her dominance and permission to control." Peggy offers no actual data or other evidence that would prove this applied broadly to all White people. Instead, she relies solely on her personal experiences.

Canada's most famous psychologist, Jordan Peterson (who has been a vocal opponent to far-left ideologies pushed in universities), mocked this paper in a speech at the University of British Columbia Free Speech Club. He states that, "McIntosh's list of privileges enjoyed by White people could apply to other races of people in different countries. This means the privileges she listed were not a function of her being White, but were more a function of being wealthy or being the majority."

An example of one of the privileges McIntosh lists is that she has "the privilege of opening a magazine or turning on the television and seeing people that look like her." To this, Jordan Peterson points out that "this is not White privilege but rather, majority privilege."

A Chinese person in China enjoys the same privileges because Chinese people are the majority in China. The same privileges exist in most countries. Growing up in Zimbabwe, most of the people I saw on television commercials on the local stations were Black. Why? Because Blacks are the majority in Zimbabwe.

Not only is this notion of White privilege academically unsound, its political purpose is also most sinister. Many would be surprised to know that it's largely derived from Marxist ideology.

Marxism proposes that, in every society, people are divided into two groups—the oppressed and the oppressors. In the case of White privilege, the villains, or oppressors, are White people. Under this notion, White people are scapegoated for many of the problems experienced by non-Whites, "the oppressed." White people are collectively branded as the oppressive hand that keeps people of color from progressing.

In this way, an entire group of people is condemned, guilted, and shamed, solely because of the color of their skin. It's hard to believe that such a dangerous ideology would be acceptable in 2020. It's become not only acceptable but celebrated, because it's an ideology that operates under the guise of helping the down-trodden. Many people fear challenging its premise, lest they be accused of being racist oppressors themselves.

When a particular ethnic group is collectively targeted and assigned universal guilt, regardless of the specific innocence or guilt of the individual, that's the textbook definition of racism. Thus, this notion of collective White privilege, which paints all White people with a broad brush, is itself deeply racist.

Oprah Winfrey recently caused a firestorm of criticism after suggesting poor and struggling Whites "still have their whiteness" and White privilege, no matter what. Many pointed to the irony of a billionaire Black woman chiding poor Whites as "privileged." In a sarcastic retort, syndicated talk radio show on Fox News Radio, Todd Starnes said, "I pray for the day that America becomes a nation where someone like Oprah will be able to become a billionaire."

VARIABLES THAT DETERMINE PRIVILEGE (HINT: BEING WHITE IS NOT ONE OF THEM)

There are many privileges that some White individuals have that are mistakenly assigned to their being White. These privileges can be due to a number of different variables, including culture, family, and economic status, which are also enjoyed by non-White races.

A. Economic and Cultural Privilege

One of the stated pieces of evidence for so-called White privilege (or its close cousin, systemic racism) touted by the left is economic disparity between Whites and minority groups. They show disparities between the median income of White households and those of Black and Hispanic households. This is true, but it is not to be considered without context. What the left invariably shows is a partial picture that focuses on disparities among White, Black, and Hispanic incomes. When we take a closer look, according to US Census Bureau data on median income by race and ethnicity from 2014, we find that there are other ethnic minority groups that earn more than White Americans.

For example, Asian Americans, Indian Americans and even Nigerian Americans, are just a few of the many ethnic minorities that out earn White Americans on average. Therefore, by omitting these other minority groups, the left is able to perpetuate the false narrative that America is designed to give only White people an unfair and underserved advantage over others.

If America is truly a system that was set up for White supremacy, then the aforementioned minority groups would not be able to outearn White people. It's clear that the economic disparities are due to variables other than White privilege.

For example, one reason Asians may be top earners is because of their cultural values. Asian cultures, in general, place a lot of emphasis on academic achievement. Many of the industries that Asian workers enter are in science and technology, fields that are typically high-earning. I suppose one could call it cultural privilege? This is a privilege that I have benefited from myself. Growing up in Zimbabwe, I come from a similar culture, where academic achievement is highly valued. That cultural background enabled me to achieve academic, career and life success.

B.   Family Privilege

There is a viral video, that purports to demonstrate White privilege. In the video, a youth counselor leads an activity/experiment with a group of young men. Some of them are Black, and some of them are White. In the video, the counselor tells the young men that they will all take part in a race. The winner, he says, will receive $100.

The counselor makes things a little more interesting with an added caveat. After the racers have lined up, he asks people to take two steps forward from the starting line, but only if they meet certain criteria.

He makes eight statements. He tells the young men to take a step forward, every time the statement applies. As he lists the criteria, the young men to whom it applies take the steps. At the end of the list, mostly all White racers are nearly to the finish line, while others, mostly the Black youth, are still at or near the original starting line.

The counselor says, "Every statement I've made, has nothing to do with anything any of you have done. It has nothing to do with the decisions you've made."

The statements the counselor makes are as follows:

- Take two steps forward if your parents are still married.
- Take two steps forward if you grew up with a father figure in the home.
- Take two steps forward if you had access to a private education.
- Take two steps forward if you had access to a free tutor growing up.
- Take two steps forward if you have never had to worry about your cellphone being shut off.
- Take two steps forward if you never had to help your mom and dad with the bills.
- Take two steps forward if it was not because of your athletic ability that you do not have to pay for college.
- Take two steps forward if you never had to wonder where your next meal was coming from.

So, as the mostly Black students are left closer to the starting line, the implication is that this race demonstrates White privilege and gives White people a competitive advantage in the race of life.

The counselor says, "I guarantee that some of these Black dudes could smoke all of you, and it's only because you have this big of a head start, that you're possibly going to win this race called life. Nothing you have done has put you in the lead you're in right now."

At the height of the George Floyd race saga, a friend of mine (who is White) posted the video of this exchange on social media and a caption asking people to start checking their White privilege.

"Is this really White privilege?" I asked her in a private message. No, it is not. I went on to explain why these eight criteria had nothing to do with race. Instead, the eight criteria are associated with a strong family structure, strong marriages, a father figure that loves and guides his children, work ethic, financial responsibility, budgeting, and socio-economic status. These attributes do not apply exclusively to White people. These attributes are shared among African, Hispanic, and Asian immigrants, for example—to a greater extent, in some cases.

Children raised in a home with a father and mother enter adulthood with more privileges than those who do not have both parents present in their lives. This has nothing to do with race, ethnicity, or sex. This is demonstrated by the fact that the poverty rate among two-parent Black families is only 7 percent. Compare that with a 22 percent poverty rate among Whites in single-parent homes. Unfortunately, in 2020, 75 percent of Black American children come from a single-parent home. Obviously, the two-parent home is the deciding privilege.

Some African Americans may find themselves at the back of the line in many of these criteria listed in the video, for cultural reasons. For example, when compared to other non-White communities, academic achievement is not rightly prioritized in most African American homes, which is a cultural issue I will discuss later. This places blacks at a disadvantage on many of the criteria mentioned in the video. But this does not mean that these are obstacles that can't be overcome by making good choices.

The video says, "We do not all start life from the same point. Others have a head start." This is true. Some people start life with a head start, and others may have more obstacles to overcome. This may sound cliché, but life is not fair. Only in a fantastical, utopian society, could we all start life with the exact same circumstances. Humanity has free will; therefore, there are enumerable sets of circumstances that people find themselves in. Some circumstances can be a direct consequence of our own choices, while others are circumstances that are beyond our control.

The parable of the talents, which the Lord Jesus Christ teaches in Matthew 25:14–30, is a perfect illustration of this fact of life.

In this parable, Jesus illustrates that in life, we do not all start out with the same amount of "talents."

The Parable of the Talents tells of a master who's leaving his estate to travel. Before he leaves, the man entrusts his estate to his servants. To each of his servants, he gives a different number of talents, to steward while he is gone. One servant receives five talents, the second receives two, and the third receives only one. They are each instructed to make use of the talents and multiply them. The first two men are shrewdly able to double their talents. While the third decides to bury the one talent he was given and do nothing with it.

Upon returning from his travels after a long absence, the master asks his three servants for an account of the talents he entrusted to them. The first and the second servants explain that they each put their talents to work. They report that they have doubled the value of the money that they were entrusted with. The two servants are rewarded.

> "His lord said unto him, Well done, good and faithful
> servant; you have been faithful over a few things,
> I will make you ruler over many things: you may
> enter into the joy of thy lord" (Matt. 25:23, NKJV).

However, out of fear, the third servant, hides his talent, burying it in the ground, for which he is severely reprimanded and punished. The one talent he has is taken from him and given to the one who had been entrusted with five talents.

I interpret this to mean that each of us has different gifts. Some have more, and others have less. Some have better circumstances than others. But we are expected to make something of what each of us has been given, no matter how big or small.

OTHER TYPES OF PRIVILEGE

It is important to note there are other variables in an individual's life that may give them privilege or advantages. For example, being physically attractive, regardless of your race, generally gives you an advantage in life. Athletic ability and intelligence are other examples. These gifts are not limited to any one race. The country you live in can certainly afford unique advantages and privilege. Living in America is a privilege for people of all races. The poorest Americans, of all races, are among the wealthiest people on the planet. We could call this "American privilege."

"Choice privilege" is a privilege you choose to have. It is privilege that is a direct result of an individual's good choices. This is something that we teach to our children, in our home, from the time they are toddlers. We have a saying in our home: "When you make good choices, good things happen." Conversely, our kids will tell you that when you make bad choices, bad things happen.

CHAPTER 2

MY STORY—GROWING UP IN AFRICA

"Be not deceived; God is not mocked: for whatsoever a man soweth, that shall he also reap" (Gal. 6:7–9, NKJV).

L ife is a decision tree. Every choice you make, big and small, determines where you end up in life. My mother always taught me that if I wanted a good life, I'd have to learn how to make good choices. Whatever your faith, there is a universal law: You reap what you sow. This principle provided me with a guiding light throughout my teen and early adulthood years, a time when the temptation to veer off the straight and narrow path was strong. I was not a perfect teen. But when I veered off the narrow path, it was never too far. The fear of reaping negative consequences always kept me on or near the path.

The biblical concept of sowing and reaping is as true today as it was when it was written thousands of years ago. Making good choices is the one thing we have individual control over. Making good choices contributes to one's success and well-being. Life will throw you some curve balls, things that are out of your control, but consistently making good choices will almost always put you on a positive trajectory in life.

When I take stock of my own life—my past, present, and future—I see that I am blessed. For my part, I live a life of great privilege, because I have made good choices for the most part. The color of my skin has never been a driving factor or a hinderance to my success in any way.

I was raised to believe that it is the value I bring to the world that will ultimately put me on a path to success. It's choosing to rise above any circumstances or obstacles that life may bring. It's adhering to the basic principles of success, like hard work and determination to achieve, that will ultimately determine my success in life.

Although my mother spoiled me in many ways, since I was her only child, she prepared me for the realities of life by speaking words of wisdom into my life. She would always tell me that life was generally hard and that to make it in life you must be intentional about everything you do. She made sure I understood that no one owed me anything, and therefore I was not entitled to anything. Two of the most powerful principles she taught me were personal responsibility and self-determination.

These guiding principles meant that there was no room for excuses and no room to assign blame to others or to our circumstances. That meant, aside from God's sovereignty over my life, I was the one ultimately in charge of my destiny. Armed with these core values, I have tried to live my life with intentionality, knowing that I will reap the harvest of the choices I make. Judging by where my life is today, I have, for the most part, made good choices. It is God to whom I give the credit and the glory for blessing me with a mother who instilled in me these life-giving values that have shaped my life.

MY STORY—GROWING UP IN POST-COLONIAL ZIMBABWE

My upbringing may offer some insight into what has shaped my perspective on the current political and social landscape in America, so I'm going to take you back to where my life began. My story begins in the early 1980s, in post-colonial Zimbabwe, in a tiny rural town called Rusape, which had just one traffic light. At the time, my mother was a twenty-one-year-old single mother and elementary school teacher. She later moved to the capital city, Harare, where she met and married my stepfather.

Prior to gaining independence in 1980, Zimbabwe (known as Rhodesia before independence) was racially segregated, in a way similar to apartheid in South Africa. Whites, who had migrated from England in the 1800s, had seized power and established a chartered state independent from the British empire. During this time, many restrictions were placed on the Black indigenous population of Zimbabwe. For example, Blacks were not allowed to live in the suburban neighborhoods. Among other restrictions, schools were segregated, and certain types of employment were reserved for Whites only.

Up until independence, my mother had lived her entire life under this colonial regime, headed then by Prime Minister Ian Smith. The colonial regime fell following a hard-fought liberation war, that forced the colonial powers to surrender.

After Zimbabwe's independence, the newly elected president, Robert Mugabe, was a hero to the people of Zimbabwe. He was the freedom fighter who had dedicated his life, fought against a racist regime, and liberated his people from colonial oppression. Indeed, he was a hero to us all at the time.

In the early years of his regime, President Mugabe received the support of Western governments in the form of development aid. He was also nominated for a Nobel Peace Prize, recognizing his efforts to bring about the Rhodesian (Zimbabwean) peace settlement.

In the early years of his regime, Mugabe pursued a policy of reconciliation with the minority White Rhodesians. He even appointed two White ministers to his government. In a speech in 1981, he said, "If yesterday I fought you as an enemy, today you have become a friend. If yesterday you hated me, today you cannot avoid the love that binds me to you."

Despite Mugabe (an avowed socialist) suggesting Zimbabwe would become a full-scale socialist state with a centralized economy, Mugabe's budgetary policies were surprisingly conservative, keeping, for the most part, the free market system established by the Ian Smith regime in place. This was a calculated move on Mugabe's part to prevent a mass exodus of Whites that would likely crash the Zimbabwean economy.

As a result of his early approach, growing up in Zimbabwe in the '80s and '90s was a beautiful experience. Mugabe's policies of reconciliation with White Zimbabweans meant there was little to no visible racial tension between Blacks and Whites. Even though my mother had grown up under the oppressive Ian Smith regime and had experienced systemic racism and discrimination firsthand, she was never bitter about the past. She barely talked about it, and if she did, it was for a brief historical reference. The past did not define her. This was true of most Zimbabweans, both Black and White, who looked to the future with hope for their new country.

I have fond memories of growing up in the capital city, Harare. Zimbabwe was a thriving country. Based on its robust agricultural exports to other African countries, it was widely known as the breadbasket of Africa. It also had a strong, internationally traded currency and a flourishing tourism industry.

Harare, also known as the "sunshine city," was a beautiful cosmopolitan city, home to people from all over the world. It had modern buildings, wide thoroughfares, and beautiful parks and gardens. Most importantly, it was said by many, to have the best weather in the world. The normal annual high temperature ranges from 72 to 82 degrees Fahrenheit, with little humidity.

Because I attended a private school that was popular with expats, I went to school with many people from all over the world: Sweden, Australia, Botswana, and even obscure places, like Yugoslavia.

Although racial segregation, mandated by the state, had ended post-independence, there were still some remnants of a segregated society. This could be seen even a decade into independence. When the schools and neighborhoods desegregated in the early 1980s, most White Zimbabweans, took their children out of the public schools and enrolled them in private schools. Private school in Zimbabwe is very expensive. At that time, they were mostly attended by Whites.

The segregation shaped up to be more of an economic and class segregation, as wealthier Black Zimbabweans, who could afford to live in northern suburbs, moved there and took their children to private schools as well.

Growing up, I lived in the northern suburbs and went to private school, so I grew up in a racially integrated society. It was not because my mother was wealthy, but because she was determined to raise me in the best neighborhood and place me in the best private schools. She worked hard to ensure that I had the best of everything.

Much like the British class system, Zimbabwe still has a very distinct class system. An abundance of cheap labor in Zimbabwe meant I grew up having domestic staff, which was typical for a middle-class family. We had a full-time maid who cooked and cleaned. We also had a full-time gardener who tended to our yard. When I visit Zimbabwe now, after having lived here in America for so long, I experience re-entry shock every time. What was normal to me growing up, I now can never get used to again—having domestic workers running around and waiting on me hand and foot.

People who work such service jobs work long hours for very little money and are akin to a peasant class. Unfortunately, this class of people has very little hope of ever lifting themselves out of that class and into another class. If you're born poor in Zimbabwe, you're almost always going to die poor. Their class system is very rigid and provides little to no opportunity for upward mobility.

Zimbabwe is not unique in this regard. This is how most of the world works. The one place that is unique is America. When I first came to America, the absence of a class system was a culture shock. I've found that people here are generally treated with equal human dignity, no matter their socio-economic status. This was foreign to me. The first time I experienced this was when I went to eat at a restaurant with my American friends and they referred to the waiter as "sir." I thought, "Sir? To a waiter?" In Zimbabwe, *sir* is reserved for people from higher classes.

Another culture shock was seeing poor and even homeless White people. In Zimbabwe, there was no such thing. So, my first impression of America was that it was a very strangely egalitarian society—a place where your race, socio-economic status, or family, didn't box you in or seal your fate, in either a good or a bad way.

EDUCATION SYSTEM

My mother, like most Zimbabwean parents, values the importance of education in shaping a child's life. When I was a child, she instilled in me the principle of working hard to excel in school.

A high bar is set for academic achievement in the Zimbabwean culture. African parents expect their children to get straight A's, and, of course, my mother was not the exception. It was highly competitive. Grades were publicly announced to the entire class, ranking each student from the first to last. Zimbabwean parents were competitive when it came to whose kids are getting the best grades. It's kind of like the way American parents are competitive with their kid's sports. Academics were our sport in Zimbabwe.

Students were also very competitive among themselves. After every test, everyone's grades were nailed to the wall on a sheet of paper for the whole class to see. You never wanted to be the one whose grade was at the bottom of the page.

After reading Candace Owen's book *Blackout*, I have learned this a major cultural difference between African culture and Black American culture. She writes, "Education is not deemed 'cool' by many Black (American) students." She goes on to say, "Being smart, getting good grades and being studious, is frowned upon."

For Zimbabweans (and Africans in general), it was quite the contrary. Excelling at school and getting good grades was considered cool. When I was a teenager, the most sought-after guys, were the ones who got the best grades.

When I was in elementary and middle school, each grade had four different class levels: A, B, C, and D. The students in class A were the best and the brightest. The students in class D were the least bright. The cool kids were always the ones in Class A. The goal of every student in the rest of the classes was to get their grades up so they could move up classes, from D to C or C to B, and ultimately be placed in class A.

This meant your spot in class A was never secure. If your grades fell, you could be moved to a lower class. This resulted in great embarrassment. The pressure for academic excellence was always on. It was reinforced by parents, teachers, and even your classmates.

Both public and private schools in Zimbabwe were very formal. Faith and God was central in both systems. Every student wore a uniform (like in Harry Potter), complete with ties for boys, long skirts for girls, blazers, socks, and school shoes, which had to be polished every morning. Having unpolished shoes at school was an offense that could land you a reprimand from a teacher or prefect. Prefects were senior students who were authorized to enforce discipline. They ensured your uniform was in full compliance.

Every morning, when the teacher entered the classroom, out of respect, all the students would stand up in concert to say, "Good morning Mrs. so and so!" Punishment for bad behavior was swift and sometimes included a swatting (in the public schools only). Once, in fifth grade, I didn't hand in my homework. For punishment, I had to spend recess in class, writing, "I must do my homework," one hundred times on the chalk board. It was brutal. After that, I never failed to turn in my homework again.

To ensure my academic performance was never lagging, every school holiday, my mother put me in tutoring classes. Of course, as a child, I resented this. But I needed it because I was not the academic type. When it came to school, my mother had to constantly push me. I hated reading. But she made me read.

Dr. Ben Carson recounts, in his book *Gifted Hands*, a similar story with his mother. She locked him and his brother up in a room and forced them to read. She would have them turn in book reports to her. The funny thing is that Dr. Carson's mom was illiterate. His story resonated with me because my mother similarly pushed me academically. In retrospect, I am so grateful she did.

I was more of an artist, and art was my favorite subject. I was also into modeling, beauty, and fashion—all the things that you can't make a serious career out of in Zimbabwe. These were paths that were generally frowned upon. Your parents, as a Zimbabwean child, expected you to choose a "serious career," like doctor, lawyer, engineer, accountant, etc. I thought I wanted to be an artist. My mother always encouraged me to be what I wanted to be, but society told me, "Being an artist will make a great hobby."

The way our education system worked was that after completing high school, a series of national exams had to be taken. If you wanted to graduate from high school and or go to college, these exams had to be passed.

Societally, these exams determined if you were going to be a winner or loser in life. So, the pressure was on. It was a big deal and a scary one.

Everything about these exams, taken over a couple of weeks, was menacing. The exam itself came from the prestigious University of Cambridge. It was special delivered from the United Kingdom. It was not administered in your own classroom or school. Large halls, in several different locations, were rented to accommodate students from all over the city.

Each student had their own desk. It was so quiet that you could literally hear a pin drop. Everyone around was a stranger, because people in your class were sent to random exam locations. There were specially hired exam monitors that quietly paced the aisles to ensure strict adherence to the rules.

Leading up to the exam, I studied hard. My mother would not even let me out of the house. Friends would come over, wanting me to go out with them. My mother would give me the choice, with a stern warning to make the right choice.

Of course, I did not want to fail. Failing would be a great embarrassment, not only for me, but for my mother. Relatives were already whispering about the likelihood of my not doing well, because I was the "free-spirited artist type" that was not to be taken seriously. This was their perception.

My mother would always lecture me, saying, "If you don't pass your exams, it's not because I didn't give you every tool and opportunity to succeed!" After all, she had sacrificed to send me to private school, which she could only afford by faith and the grace of God. So I was not about to let my mother down.

Waiting for the results was the worst part because it took two months to get them. It was the longest and worse two months of any teen's life in Zimbabwe! The day the results arrived, I was a nervous wreck. This was it. Was I going to disappoint my mother and give my snarky relatives the satisfaction of being right? Was I going to be a failure in life?

I can vividly remember the day I went to my school to pick up my exam results. The grades came in a neat, special envelope with a seal that read, CAMBRIDGE UNIVERSITY. They handed over the results, and I shakingly opened the envelope, heart in throat. I pulled out the paper, and I could not believe my eyes—five A's and two B's. Was this for real? Even I was surprised at how well I did. I was jubilant! My mother and I jumped up and down for joy. I did it. It was an early sign that I was going to have a bright and successful future.

In retrospect, I realize, every aspect of my early education helped shape me to be the person I am today. Even seemingly insignificant things, like having to polish my shoes every morning before school, taught me how to take pride in how I present myself to the world. I learned to respect authority. The competitive nature of our education system prepared me for the real world and for competing in the workforce to get ahead.

These are just a few examples of how my childhood in Zimbabwe shaped my perspective on life, my choices, and, ultimately, my destiny in America.

CHAPTER 3

GOD'S CHOICE—
COMING TO AMERICA

For most of my childhood, Zimbabwe was a stable, financially sound, and safe nation. It was not until the early to mid-1990s that things began to fall apart. Because I was young at the time, it was only in retrospect of studying historical accounts, that the full understanding of the events that took place came into my view.

Despite his early successes, President Mugabe's reputation as a visionary leader began to tarnish. According to historical accounts, the President became increasingly paranoid and he began to go after political rivals to centralize his power. The early '90s gave rise to a new political elite, as Mugabe, his ministers, and loyalists, would flaunt their wealth by living extravagant lifestyles.

Their wealth was partially derived from the acquisition of lucrative commercial farms. Farms that had been expropriated from White farmers at below market prices. This occurred, in breach of the Lancaster House Agreement, signed at the time of independence. Mugabe shifted away from the free-market economy and began to implement policies that would centralize and socialize the economy.

By the late 1990s, Zimbabwe's once bustling economy had declined to the point that many Black Zimbabweans were arguably worse off than they were prior to independence. Life expectancy had dropped to record lows, unemployment was on the rise, and real wages were lower.

Feeling cornered, Mugabe's rhetoric toward White Zimbabweans began to change. He began to blame the country's economic woes on the White Zimbabwean minority and continued to double down on seizures of White-owned commercial farms.

The farm seizures devastated Zimbabwe's economy. Agricultural productivity plummeted and caused a food crisis in the nation. Suddenly, 75 percent of Zimbabwe's population found itself having to rely on US food-aid, as the GDP dropped by 50 percent.

Due to a decrease in tax revenue and a sharp decline in agricultural exports, Mugabe's regime began an unprecedented series of quantitative easing measures, aka "money printing," which led to the crash of the Zimbabwean dollar. Inflation rates soared to 7600 percent in 2007. One year later, the inflation rate had reached a staggering 250 million percent. At the time, a single loaf a bread cost two-thirds of a day's wages. Unemployment soured to 80 percent, and life expectancy dropped to thirty-four years old, a sharp decline from the 1997 expectancy of sixty-three years old.

In 2000, during the start of the inflation, I was graduating high school. We would spend hours every day in three-mile long lines, just to get a tank of gasoline in our car. The shelves at the grocery stores were totally empty. You had to buy basic food items on the black market. An industry of food brokers and dealers, with access to farmers, emerged and became the only source for most foods. Bread was subsidized by the government. Every morning, people would line up at six o'clock, before the supermarket opened, to get the daily batch of bread that would arrive. By nine o'clock, bread would be sold out, and you would have to try your luck the next day.

My mother lost her entire life savings overnight. Imagine waking up, only to find out that the $200,000 in your retirement account can now buy you a bag of groceries. It was a traumatic time, and things only got worse. Inflation got so bad that Zimbabwe printed a one-hundred-trillion-dollar note. Converted to USD, it was worth five bucks, just enough to buy a loaf of bread.

GOING TO AMERICA BY FAITH

After their children graduate from high school, it's customary for most middle-class Zimbabweans to send them to study abroad. The main reason is because there are only two major universities in Zimbabwe, and only the best and brightest are accepted to them. But as Zimbabwe began to decline, studying abroad became a reason for me to escape the desperate situation in search of opportunity.

A few years prior to my graduation from high school, I had visited Florida and California with my church's youth group. I was blown away by America. It was everything that I expected it would be and more. It was just like in the movies we watched growing up.

We visited Florida and California, where we were hosted by American families. We got to experience what life was like for an American family on a day-to-day basis. One of the cultural differences that I found fascinating was the fact that meals were very informal. There was no designated breakfast time, when everyone gathered to eat breakfast together as a family. In Zimbabwe, meals are a lot more formal; breakfast, lunch, and dinner are family events. On the weekends, we would eat an English breakfast: eggs, bacon, baked beans, fried tomato, and toast.

In contrast, in America I remember waking up and eating pop tarts, candy bars, and cereal for breakfast. When I was seventeen, all this was heavenly.

Dinnertime in America was also very casual. A few times, we ordered fast food from a drive-thru, something I had never seen before. I thought it was a brilliant concept.

Two years after this visit, I graduated from high school. Now it was time to select a university. Most Zimbabweans tend to go to the UK, Canada, Australia, or the States for university. My heart was set on going back to America. Of course, with all the economic turmoil that was going on in the country, this was a pipe dream. After losing her life savings in the economic collapse, my mother didn't have the kind of money it would take to send me to school in America. But because my mother is a woman of faith, she declared God would make a way where there seemed to be no way. She was desperate for me to escape the despair that had gripped our nation. We took a step of faith, believing God would somehow make a way for me.

I started applying to universities in the United States. Cornell and Virginia Tech were my top choices. After months of going back and forth with the universities, I was not getting anywhere. A year passed, and it felt like I had just been going in circles, submitting applications and documents via snail mail, only to be told I was missing something.

In 2001, email, internet and personal computers were still somewhat of a novel luxury in Zimbabwe. I didn't have a computer at home. So, I would get on the bus and ride into town to the United States Library. There, I would use the computer and internet to communicate with the universities. After almost a year with no success, despair was starting to set in. All my friends had already left to study abroad.

I felt stuck. But my mother, who is a woman of faith and a prayer warrior, always encouraged me and told me not give up on my dream. I continued to go back to the US Library to read American literature and use the internet to research other universities.

One afternoon, an American woman that worked at the library said she had an application from to a university in the Midwest. She said she knew the university to be very responsive and that it even offered an international student scholarship. Given my financial circumstances, I desperately needed financial aid. In retrospect, this was destiny. The first week after arriving in America, I would meet my future husband.

Reluctantly, I applied and submitted the paperwork. In comparison to the other schools I applied to, I was shocked at how quickly they responded. They accepted my application and awarded me a partial scholarship. That was an amazing moment. Finally, a breakthrough!

During that pivotal moment in my life, Zimbabwe's economic woes were only intensifying. This meant that my mother could no longer request US dollars from the bank to purchase my plane ticket. The Reserve Bank of Zimbabwe had run out of foreign currency. The only foreign currency that was available was found on the black market for thousands of percentage points above the official rate.

Even though my faith began to wane, my mother was steadfast in her faith that God would make a way. This gave me hope. We came up with creative ways to raise money to buy foreign currency from individuals. That December, shortly after Christmas, my mother hosted a fund-raising dinner event with friends and family. We managed to raise enough money to buy my ticket. She ran into an old friend who offered to sell her foreign currency at the official rate. This was another breakthrough and miracle.

By faith, without knowing how I was going to pay for my tuition, I chose to get on the plane to Kansas City, with nothing but a suitcase, and $300 in my pocket.

When I landed, it was freezing cold and there was snow on the ground. I had never seen snow, and I'd never experienced cold weather. Luckily, the day before I left Zimbabwe, one of my mother's friends who had visited cold climates, donated her coat to me. The coat was a black faux fur coat that was about five sizes too big. I looked like I was drowning it in every time I wore it.

Upon arriving in the US, I was met by a couple of Christian college girls. They had a ministry that housed international students until they got on their feet. I lived with them for a couple of months, while I looked for a place to stay and an on-campus job.

Within a couple of months, I found a job on campus and was renting a room in a house with other students. At nineteen years old, for the first time, I was on my own, paying rent and being responsible for myself. I had to brainstorm on how I was going to pay for my tuition fees. The scholarship only covered the out-of-state fees. So, I had to figure out how I was going to pay my way through college.

To keep my partial scholarship, I had to maintain a 3.5 GPA. I worked at the campus gym, where I made just about enough money to pay for my room and my fifty-cent packets of Raman noodles for dinner.

I went through several semesters of school, each time registering for the next semester by faith. Somehow (by miracle), I was able to register, even though I had an outstanding balance on my account. I found favor with the lady at the cashier's office. She was sympathetic to my situation in Zimbabwe and allowed me to make small payments toward the tuition fees.

After a year of college, I had accrued quite a bit of debt with the university. I knew I needed to find another way to get my tuition covered. I chose to search for additional scholarships and grants. They had all kinds of scholarships—based on merit, race, gender, etc. But there was one big problem. To qualify for the scholarships, you had to be an American citizen. This automatically disqualified me.

After sharing my dilemma with another international student, I found a potential solution. This roommate was the manager of a sports team. For this, she received a scholarship to pay her tuition. After meeting with several of the sports coaches, I found favor with the track and field coach, and on the spot, he offered me a job as a track manager. This was divine providence because he already had a manager. He decided to add me on as a second manager for the team anyway. In the history of the university, this was the first time a sports team had two managers. This had to be the hand of God as I found favor.

The first day on my job as track manager, it didn't take long for me to realize that the job wasn't as prestigious as it sounded. I basically did the coach's dirty work—stuff he didn't want to do. But I didn't mind. My school fees were covered, so I chose to be the best track manager I could be.

Being a track manager meant that I would spend thirty-plus hours per week in practices and traveling with the team to track meets.

I had to work thirty-plus hours a week to take care of myself. As an international student, I also had to stay enrolled in school full-time.

For the last two years of college, I worked diligently thirty-plus hours per week as a track manager, thirty hours a week at my job, and fifteen credit hours of college classes. My schedule was packed. I had no time to party or socialize with other college students, who seemed to have a lot of time on their hands.

Coming from Zimbabwe, where academic excellence is required, it was a bit of culture shock to see how Americans were fine with doing the bare minimum to get through school. Many of my classmates were happy to just get a passing grade. Two of my African friends and I were always at the top of our class. We had to make A's. There was even a silent competition between the three of us for who got the highest grades.

Between track practice, track meets, working, school, and late-night study, it was a tough period in my life. But I pressed forward and persevered. I didn't even own a car for the entire four years I was in college. I walked everywhere, in all kinds of weather, including snow blizzards.

Looking back at that difficult period of my life, I realize it helped develop who I am today, in a positive way. It humbled me and taught me how to be resilient and disciplined.

Coming to America and having to provide for myself made me realize that, as an only child in Zimbabwe, I had been so spoiled. My mother had always worked hard to provide a great life for me. We lived in the smallest house in the wealthiest neighborhood. I went to private school with children of the wealthy and the elites of Harare.

I grew up always having domestic workers around me that did my laundry, cleaned, and cooked meals for me. This is not because we were wealthy but because labor is so cheap in Zimbabwe. The average middle-class family can afford to have a full-time maid, nanny, cook, gardener, and even a driver. The average wage for each of these domestic workers is only $5 per day. After coming to America, I had to learn how to do basic things, like wash my own clothes and cook for myself for the first time.

MEETING MY HUSBAND

Within a few weeks of being on campus, Michael had spotted me. I was a new freshman, and he was in his second year of doctoral school. He pursued me for an entire year, trying to get a date, but I wouldn't give in.

Michael was White. In Zimbabwe, White guys just never dated Black girls. So this was new to me. Honestly, I had prejudice about dating a White guy. I thought, "What would I have in common with a White person? I like hip hop, and he probably likes rock music."

After he'd pursued me for a year, I stopped hearing from Michael. I had stopped working at the campus gym where I would normally see him. I had moved to a different apartment, so the landline number he had for me was no longer valid. He thought I had gone back to Zimbabwe.

One winter, after Christmas break, I got a job as hostess at a restaurant. On my first day as the hostess, I was told to go and put a magnet next to the name of one of the servers—Michael—to signal he had a new table. I went to the back to do just that, and low and behold, it was my Michael.

Looking back, I know God put me right back in front of him. This time, I could not escape his plan. Knowing how he had so patiently and diligently tried to get a date with me for so long, I finally agreed to go out with him. I fell in love with him on the first date. All my preconceived ideas about him were wrong. We had so much in common. He loved hip hop music too.

All this happened in my second year of college. A few months after we had started dating, Michael graduated. We dated for the next three years, while I finished college. Even though I was a poor college student, and he was now working full-time, I remained independent. I never expected a hand-out from my boyfriend.

Although it was nice when he took me out to fancy dinners or occasionally bought me a nice Coach purse.

After I graduated from college, Michael proposed to me. In June we got married in a small wedding outside of the new house that he had just built for us, with a beautiful back drop of the downtown skyline. We were married five years before we had children. We spent a lot of time travelling the world—from Hong Kong to Europe to South Africa and more.

EARLY CAREER AND BUSINESS

After graduating with my bachelor's degree in business administration, I was hired by a big bank. I worked at an entry-level position as a customer service agent for 401Ks managed by the bank. Within a few months of being hired, I applied for a better position and was promoted to become a financial advisor representative. I had to study and pass a series of exams that are required by the SEC to become a financial advisor.

It was like going back to school, reading volumes of books to pass exams. I pressed through, studying at night when I got off work, and I passed all the exams flying colors.

After three years of working in corporate America, e-commerce and eBay had just started to take off in a big way. Because of my entrepreneurial spirit, in my spare time, I chose to start selling all kinds of stuff on eBay. My goal was always to start my own business.

When I was six years old, my mother had left her teaching job and started a small business, manufacturing and retailing her own line of cane furniture. I always admired my mother for owning her own business. I knew that was the path I was going to end up on.

After trying many different side businesses over the years, I landed on a women's beauty product. The product had just burst onto the scene and was hot. It was the perfect time to enter the market. There was little competition and high demand for the product. Shortly after migrating my side business from eBay to my own website, my business exploded.

At the time, I would work my 9-to-5 job, then come home to answer emails from customers and ship orders out of my spare bedroom. Within a few of months, I was making more money working part-time in my spare bedroom than I was working as a financial advisor for a prestigious bank. I put in my two weeks' notice, hired an assistant, and began working to make my business grow. Within a year, at the age of twenty-seven, I had a business that was grossing over a million dollars in sales and employed five people.

At the age of twenty-eight, I had graduated college, married my college sweetheart, worked a good job in corporate America, started a successful small business, lived in a beautiful home, and was traveling the world. A couple of years later, my husband and I started our family. We are now parents to three beautiful (but noisy) children. My husband always jokes that they're easy on the eyes but hard on the ears.

CHOICES

God has truly, "blessed me abundantly above all that I could have ever asked for or could have imagined" (Eph. 3:20, NKJV).

Every other year, my husband and I and our children fly to Zimbabwe to visit. Each time we travel to the mountains, we pass through Rusape, the small town where I was born. We drive past the small, now dilapidated hospital I was born in. This small, remote, rural town is where my life began. Every time we drive past it, I marvel at my humble beginnings and how far the Lord has taken me.

It started with my mother making the choice to leave that small town to find a better life for herself and her child. I often wonder what my life would have been like had my mother been paralyzed by victimhood and a lack of drive for a better life. She had every excuse to be a victim. At the age of twenty-one, she had recently become an orphan, when her mother tragically died from a sudden illness. Her father died in a tragic car accident when she was only nine years old. All her life up until this point had been spent under the oppressive Smith Regime, which made her a second-class citizen in her own country. And now, she found herself a new single mother.

My father was an illegal immigrant from Mali who had to constantly be on the run from Zimbabwean immigration officers. Illegal immigration in Zimbabwe is a serious crime. Eventually, to evade immigration officers, my father had to escape to neighboring Zambia. He recently told me he literally tried to swim across the crocodile and hippo infested Zambezi river to evade customs and border control in Zambia.

The relationship between my mother and father never really worked out. My mother put herself through teacher's college and became an elementary school teacher. Teachers are not paid very well in Zimbabwe. So my mother always had a side hustle. During school holidays, we would take the train to neighboring South Africa so she could buy high demand goods to import for resale.

She later stopped teaching and started her own vertically integrated custom furniture business. She had workers that made the furniture, and she also had a retail store. On weekends, my mother and I were at trade shows exhibiting her furniture. With that business, she was able to provide a decent life for us and put me through private school, which provided me with a strong educational foundation and helped shape my life. She also raised me to know the Lord, which turned out to be one of the best gifts she gave me.

My story is about putting my faith in my creator, making good choices, working hard, and having determination. In all that I have been able to achieve in life, being Black, has not been an impediment, either in Zimbabwe or here in America. I cherish the fact that my mother raised me to see the world through the lens of being a child of God, with a unique purpose and destiny. She did not raise me to see the world through the lens of my skin color. That one factor alone makes a world of difference in how one perceives the world. The latter world view is limiting, while the former is infinite and liberating.

This is the attitude I brought to America. I came to America to take advantage of every opportunity there is and with a purpose — to make something of myself. This is the same attitude that most African immigrants have when they come to America.

Generally, African immigrants feel privileged to be one of the relatively few to make it to this great country. We are grateful because many of us come from countries where there is very little to no opportunities for people to advance. There aren't a lot of places in the world that provide a ladder from poverty to success. That's what makes America so unique and great.

Only to America can you come with nothing but a suitcase, like I did, and in seven short years own a successful business that employs several people. For me, this has truly been the land of opportunity.

That is why the narrative that America is a systemically racist and oppressive nation is a total farce to me. I can assure you that millions of Africans would love to take the place of any so-called progressives that peddles this fantasy. The truth is, there is no place like America. This country has its flaws, but it is truly an exceptional nation. Being born in the U.S.A., no matter what color you are, is a privilege all in itself.

In America, three simple life choices nearly always guarantee you a decent life. A research study done by Ron Haskins, at the Brookings Institute, found that the likelihood of economic success was dependent on achieving what he called the "success sequence," which is:

1. Graduate from high school
2. Maintain a full-time job or have a partner who does
3. Have children while married and after age twenty-one

Of course, the outcomes of this sequence will vary from person to person based on a number of variables, some of which may be beyond the person's control. Notice the success sequence is based on personal choices and *not* the color of one's skin.

My husband has been equally successful, having put himself through school and then going on to be a successful real estate investor. He grew up in a poor family and was also raised by a single mother. He has had to work hard to overcome many obstacles for everything he has achieved. He had no White privilege. What he did have was the determination to overcome the poverty he grew up experiencing. He made good choices, worked hard, and did things in the right order. Daily, he continues to work hard and be a man who strives to give his family the best life possible. Marrying him was one of the best choices I ever made.

We both started our early adulthoods with nothing but have been able to be build a great life together. We prioritize our lives with the biblical values of faith, family, country, and work. We chose to work hard and prioritize education. We chose to pursue and maintain jobs and ultimately own our own businesses. We chose to get married first before having children, inadvertently following the success sequence to the T.

The success sequence and choices alone would not lead to success without a free society and a free-market system that provides equal opportunity as a ladder from a lower class to as high as you are willing to go. America is uniquely such a society. This is one of the things that make America truly exceptional. Therefore, coming to America was among the best choices I have made in life.

CHAPTER 4

BLACK AMERICA, RACE, AND THE DEMOCRATIC PARTY

As a teenager growing up in Zimbabwe, I always admired Black Americans from afar. In many ways, I still have great admiration for Black Americans, for the contributions they've made to American culture by way of music, sports, movies, comedy, and Christian spirituality. When I was growing up, most of the entertainment consumed in Zimbabwe, came from America. As a teen, my favorite shows were the *Fresh Prince of Bel Air*, *The Cosby Show*, and *Family Matters*. Shows like these formed my opinion of Black Americans. When I was a teen, my peers and I emulated Black Americans.

When I came to the United States for the first time in 2003, race was rarely ever a topic of the conversation in my circle or on the news. If there were racial tensions, they didn't dominate the news cycles like they do now.

It wasn't until President Obama's second term that I began to notice the racial narrative heating up. Despite his promise to bring racial unity during his campaign, President Obama did more to fan the flames of racial tension than extinguish them. He is the first prominent person I noticed tacitly promoting the idea that America was a systemically racist country.

Since then, this idea has not only dominated the political conversation but has become embedded in every sphere of American society.

As a Black woman whose American experience directly contradicts the assertion that America is systemically racist, I chose to take a closer look at Black American history. I wanted to make sense of this relatively new era in American politics, where race and identity has become central to all aspects of life.

This chapter takes you through the shocking discoveries that I have made while exploring Black American history. I expose how the progressive left uses identity (race) politics as a political weapon to gain power. While the left poses as champions for Black Americans, their policies are the guiding force in the systematic dismantling of the pillars that held Black society up.

They scapegoat White privilege and White supremacy as the reasons why the Black community is in the state it's in now. In doing so, they divert the discussion away from the root causes of the systematic decline of the Black community. Much in the same way, self-avowed Socialist President Mugabe of Zimbabwe began to blame White farmers for the economic woes caused by his own Socialist policies. The left is using the very same playbook. To fight back against this attempt to create racial disunity, we must understand how Black America got to where it is today.

Historically, Black Americans have sustained a lot of trauma throughout their history. Because of the long and hard-fought struggle for equality, there is a deep wound that developed over many decades that has not been allowed to heal. There are those who benefit politically from keeping these wounds from healing. Exploiting this vulnerability has worked well for them, both financially and politically. So why would they want it any other way?

The Democratic Party relies heavily on the Black vote to win elections. To win elections, the Dems need between 90 and

94 percent of the Black vote. Since 1965, the Democratic party has routinely gotten these kinds of numbers, giving them a near monopoly on the Black vote.

But what has it gotten the Black community? After almost exclusively voting for Democrats, for over fifty years, Black America has declined on almost every major metric. The Democratic Party has not only failed to deliver for Black America but has created policies that are detrimental. In exchange for their monolithic voting block, the Black community has received policies that have led to poverty, dependence on handouts, abortion mills to exterminate their unborn, and destruction of the Black family unit.

Despite this, the Democrats continue to secure the vast majority of the Black vote year after year. How is this even possible? Every election cycle, the Democratic Party and the media (which are one in the same) manage to convince Black Americans that the number one issue they face is systemic racism. In doing so, they are able to take the focus away from the real issues (typically a direct result of their own failed policies) that are affecting the Black community.

Based on my research, most of the ails of the Black community—from the disparity in wealth to teen pregnancy to crime—can be traced back to a number of significant changes that occurred in the Black community in the 1960s. The top two changes are:

1. Incentivized removal of the father figure from the Black family.
2. Culture: A nonorganic cultural shift and the fall of the church as the central guiding force in the Black community.

The cascade of events started in the mid-1960s, following the election of Democratic President Lyndon Baines Johnson (LBJ).

His "progressive" policies were the flash point in the decline we see in the Black community today.

BLACK PEOPLE AND THEIR MARRIAGE TO THE DEMOCRATIC PARTY

Black Americans endured some of the most inhumane atrocities during the time of slavery, and later, during segregation and Jim Crow. Ironically, this was largely at the hands of the Democratic Party, the same party that Black Americans have entrusted with their vote almost exclusively. The Democratic Party was the party of slavery and the KKK. But somehow, they managed to rewrite history and pin their evil deeds on the Republican Party, which, in reality, was founded to help Black Americans gain their freedom.

The Democrats of today will say the parties switched. This switch never happened. The Democratic Party never changed ideology; the only thing that changed was their strategy.

In the 1960s, the Democratic Party made a calculated political push to acquire the Black vote. The presidential election of 1964 was the defining moment. In 1964, we saw the shift of Black Americans to the Democratic Party. LBJ won the election, with an overwhelming 94 percent of the Black vote, with Goldwater carrying a paltry 6 percent. The reasons for this are interesting.

Despite being a known racist, known to use the N-word profusely, and helping to bury the 1957 Civil Rights Bill, LBJ signed the 1964 Civil Rights Act, as well as the 1965 Voting Rights Act. Even though Republicans were the ones at the helm, pushing these laws through, LBJ ultimately got the credit for signing them into law.

It was the Senate Republicans, led by Everett Dirksen, that championed and enabled the Civil Rights Act to pass. Everett Dirksen, a Republican from Illinois, received an award from the

NAACP for shepherding the Civil Rights Act through the legislative process. Also, a greater percentage of Republicans voted for the Civil Rights Act than Democrats did. This is all information that has been buried in history.

Because it was LBJ who ultimately signed the bill, the Civil Rights Act was perceived as an effort on the part of the Democrats. The perception created a narrative. This narrative has caused the Black community to credit that historic event to the Democratic Party. These two monumental laws, the Civil Rights Act and the Voting Rights Act, permanently endeared LBJ and the Democratic Party to Black voters.

LBJ was said to be a cold and calculating politician that spoke publicly in favor of Civil Rights during the 1960s. But he was privately known to state his true intentions and feelings toward the bill. According to LBJ's biography, written by his speech writer, Richard Goodwin, LBJ made this statement to Senator Richard Russel, Jr. (D-GA) regarding the Civil Rights Act of 1957:

"These Negroes, they're getting pretty uppity these days and that's a problem for us since they've got something now they never had before, the political pull to back up their uppityness. Now we've got to do something about this. We've got to give them a little something, just enough to quiet them down, not enough to make a difference. For if we don't move at all, then their allies will line up against us and there'll be no way of stopping them, we'll lose the filibuster and there'll be no way of putting a brake on all sorts of wild legislation. It'll be Reconstruction all over again."

In another book, *Inside the White House*, Robert MacMillan, an Air Force One steward, quotes LBJ saying to two governors, following the passage of the Civil Rights Act of 1964:

"I'll have those N*ggers voting Democrat for two hundred years!"

THE BREAKDOWN OF THE BLACK FAMILY

According to Thomas Sowell, "The Black family, which had survived centuries of slavery and discrimination, began rapidly disintegrating in the liberal welfare state that subsidized unwed pregnancy and changed welfare from an emergency rescue to a way of life."

After consolidating the Black vote, LBJ and the Democratic Party went to work, implementing policies that would lead to a breakdown of the Black family and, ultimately, the community.

One such policy that has been a giant and colossal failure is the Great Society Act of 1964. LBJ's so-called war on poverty created the social welfare programs of today. The stated goal was "the total elimination of poverty and racial injustice."

Racial injustice. Where have we heard that before? Like everything progressives promote, it sounds great. Who could argue against ending poverty and racial injustice? But the effects of this program did just the opposite.

These programs were massively promoted to Black people. The result was the separation of work from income and making men redundant (nonessential). A campaign to recruit people into the welfare system was underway. Marriage rates began to drop rapidly, because Black women were incentivized not to marry Black men. Marriage disqualified the women from being eligible to receive these new government handouts. In effect, many Black women married the government. The government provided for the family.

Consequently, millions of Black men willingly abdicated their positions and responsibilities as providers for their families. Social workers (mostly White women) visited the Black homes on a regular basis to monitor compliance and adherence to the rules surrounding welfare, and the white social workers became the new managers of the Black home.

In a short span of four years following the passage of the Great Society Act, millions of Black people flooded into the welfare system at a time when unemployment for Black people was less than 4 percent. Right around this time, progressive movements were widely introduced into the Black community and American society at large. These progressive movements challenged the nuclear family as Eurocentric and racist. At the same time, the feminist movement and Black power movement were also gaining prominence.

THE FATHERLESS GENERATION

Black author and researcher Larry Elder has said that the top three biggest problems facing the Black community are:

1) Lack of fathers in the home
2) Lack of fathers in the home
3) Lack of fathers in the home

In 1965, when the Great Society began, the out-of-wedlock birthrate among the Black community was 21 percent. At that time, this rate was considered alarming. Fast forward to 2017, when this figure had risen to a whopping 77 percent. The rate is as high as 80 percent in some cities, and most of the unwed mothers are teenagers. The Black American community is now entering the third generation of single parenthood as the norm. This is something that can be directly attributed to the passage of the Great Society Act.

The progressive culture, coupled with Democratic Party policies, has normalized the removal of the Black father from the home. The Black man's power and influence in the home and the community has been significantly reduced. In its place, we find rampant single motherhood, and the government has become the "daddy."

The effects of fatherlessness have been documented to be devastating, not only on an individual basis but to a civil society.

According to the 2017 US Census Bureau, children who come from a home without a father are:

- 4 times at greater risk of poverty
- 7 times more likely to become pregnant as a teen
- 2 times more likely to drop out high school
- 2 times greater risk of infant mortality
- More likely to go to prison
- More likely to commit crime
- More likely to abuse alcohol and drugs

Clearly, these effects are felt in the Black community. There is a "father factor" in nearly all of the societal ills we see in the Black community today.

Having a female as the head of a household, whether Black or White, generally leads to poverty, dependency, and many associated problems. One of the best-kept secrets is the fact that the poverty rate among Black married couples has been in single digits since 1994. That means marriage cuts poverty by more than half.

During the first years of my childhood, I was raised by a single mother. Fortunately, my mother later married my stepfather, which provided me a father-figure during the years that it is was critical.

Although the situation is less than ideal, I believe single mothers can and do raise children into respectable and responsible members of the society. I do, however, believe there is good reason God ordained a mother and father to raise children together.

Each parent brings a unique contribution to a child's life. These contributions are critical to a child's development.

Fathers particularly play a crucial role in shaping a son's life. A mother may not be equipped to provide the paternal connection a boy needs to develop into a man. When that connection is absent from the home, young men will turn elsewhere for that male connection. Too often, young Black men fill the void left by a missing father figure with the male comradery of gang membership. What we've often seen happen in poor Black communities is that the boys will find the male connection in nefarious characters like the neighborhood drug dealer. Thus, they're groomed into a life crime.

These are some of the root causes of problems in the Black community that rarely receive meaningful discussion by mainstream academia, media, or politics. Instead, the conversation has been dumbed down to the two most popular scapegoats: systemic racism and White supremacy.

The left has routinely promoted the idea that the societal ills of the Black community are the legacy of slavery, segregation, and Jim Crow laws. In his book *The Negro Family: The Case for National Action*, Daniel Patrick Moynihan, a Democrat and sociologist who worked in the Lyndon B. Johnson administration, detailed the breakdown of the Black family and attributed it to the legacy of slavery. However, I found that history tells a different story.

In researching and learning Black American history, I found that there is large time period that goes unnoticed and has been largely forgotten. When most people think of Black history, they think of the period of slavery and then jump right into the Civil Rights era of the 1960s. The period of Black history that is largely ignored falls between the end of slavery and the beginning of the civil rights era in late '50s and '60s.

During this time, despite having little to no representation in government, and despite having to endure systemic racism that was enshrined in the law, many Black Americans lived in thriving and successful communities.

From the end of slavery, up until the 1940s, the Black community had the highest marriage rate of any group in America. Intact families and the church were the fabric of society. Jason Riley, a Black American author and researcher, wrote this of this period in history:

"During slavery, its immediate aftermath, and on through the first quarter of the 20th century, the vast majority of Black children were raised in a two-parent household; Black marriages were as long lasting and stable as the marriages of economically comparable Whites; and the Black female-headed homes that did exist tended to be, like their White counterparts, comprised of older widows, not teenagers raising children alone."

Business formations among African Americans was high. One unintended benefit of segregation was that it forced members of the Black community to build their own industries. Because a Black person could not go to White dentist or a White restaurant, for example, Black communities were forced to build their own. Thus, Black people built their own dental schools, hotels, hospitals, movie theatres, etc.

If Black Americans were thriving and were able to accomplish all this, despite the racially unjust system that was in place during this period, then we can't attribute today's disparities seen in the Black community to the legacy of slavery. Other variables must be at play.

In his book *The Black Family in Slavery and in Freedom*, Herbert Gutman, professor of history at the Graduate Center of the City University of New York, wrote, "If enslavement caused the widespread development among Afro-Americans of 'a fatherless' matrifocal family (headed by single mothers) then such a condition should have been even more common among urban Afro-Americans closer to the time of slavery."

Simply put, the fall the Black family and the subsequent decline of their community was a later phenomenon and, therefore, had little, if anything, to do with slavery. It has been documented that the Great Society Act, was the catalyst for the decline in marriages. When government gets involved in "helping" Black people, the results have never yielded what they purported to achieve.

Jason Riley wrote an entire book called *Please Stop Helping Us*, in which he details how well-intentioned welfare programs are in fact holding Black Americans back. In theory these efforts are intended to help poor minorities, but in practice, they become massive barriers to moving forward.

A Black American friend of mine recently told me she hardly knows anyone who's married. To my astonishment, she went on to say she's never attended a wedding. When I was growing up in Zimbabwe, I felt like I went to a wedding just about every week. Marriage is that common in Zimbabwe. In fact, if you're not married by a certain age, people in the community may start to chatter. You may find that your parents, aunts, and uncles will try to take matters into their own hands and love match you with anyone and everyone they can find for you.

CULTURE

Culture and cultural upbringing play important roles in shaping a person's mind-set, attitude, and perception, and it can ultimately shape a person's destiny. There is a strong argument to be made for how culture contributes to so-called privilege.

This can be seen when considering the disparities between African immigrants and Black Americans when it comes to marriage, income, and other success indicators.

We are of the same race, but what sets us apart are cultural differences. To ascertain how these differences in culture are yielding different outcomes for Black immigrants, we need to look at how Black Americans are negatively affected by what they're told is Black American culture.

When I study Black American history, I find that, up until the late '60s, their culture was very similar to African culture. Something changed in the '60s, and a Black subculture emerged that would soon become mainstream. This relatively new culture is at the root many of the problems within the Black community, in my opinion. At its core, this culture has rejected the institutions of marriage, family, education, Judeo-Christian values, and morality. Ironically, these are the same values that built up the Black community during Reconstruction, after slavery ended.

Much of Black culture, going back to the days of slavery, has been centered around family and the church, even more so than White culture. At a critical turning point, as progressive ideology gained a foothold in the Black American community, Black culture underwent a massive transformation. After studying this period of transformation, I see that it appears to line up with the same time that Black Americans began overwhelmingly voting for and identifying themselves with the Democratic Party and liberalism.

A new Black subculture emerged. The virtues of family, hard-work, and personal responsibility began to be eroded from Black culture.

In his book *Black Rednecks and White Liberals*, Thomas Stowell writes, "The notion of the 'ghetto Black' as the authentic Black, not only spread among both White and Black intellectuals, it had social repercussions far beyond the intellectuals. Rooting

Black identity in a counter-productive culture, not only reduced incentives to move beyond that culture, it cut-off those within that culture from other blacks who had advanced beyond it, who might otherwise had been sources of examples, knowledge and experience that could have been useful to those less fortunate. But more successful blacks were being depicted as irrelevant non-members of the Black community or even as traitors to it."

Today, we see this idea of "authentic Blackness" being perpetuated. It is identified by a set characteristic you must possess to prove you are authentically Black. For example, speaking proper English is frowned upon as "talking White."

After the breakdown of the family and marriage in the Black community, the progressive left elevated the Black entertainers and athletes to be the new role models in Black society. Meanwhile, true Black leaders to be emulated, like Dr. Ben Carson, a neurosurgeon, is mocked as an Uncle Tom and a sellout. Even though he is a Black man who overcame great obstacles, including poverty, and is the first man to separate conjoined twins at the head. He is just another example of an accomplished Black man routinely mocked by the liberal media. Taking its cues from the media, the Black community generally rejects him as a leader.

Thug culture and songs like Cardi B's "WAP" (which stands for "wet a*s pu**y) reinvent ways to glorify a life of crime and sexual promiscuity. This culture is glorified in modern rap music. In being promoted on radio, television, the internet, and social media, this counterfeit culture is intentionally force-fed to members of the Black community as the measure of their blackness.

In her bestselling book *Blackout*, Candace Owens laments the cultural shift that has taken place in Black music. She discusses the way Black music has changed for the worse since the days of her grandfather. Back in his day, Black-owned Motown records represented numerous soulful Black artists who sang about love and family. By contrast, today's music has ventured far from that wholesome picture.

Furthermore, Candace Owens writes, "Our culture today is much about achieving a status of 'coolness' through the slow decay of morality: less clothing, more profanity, less education.... An artist would be hard pressed to land a number one track singing about family and love. Those days of Black America are long gone."

The counterfeit Black culture being sold to Black Americans as the hallmarks of their blackness erodes the moral fabric of the society. In more ways than one, it has done a lot of harm to the Black community. It has perpetuated negative stereotypes that cause others to be prejudiced against Black people. It has also fostered a cultural attitude that is not conducive to success.

If it's not enough that the counterfeit culture is being shaped by entertainment, it is also being amplified by progressive ideologues in every sphere of society.

The National Museum of African American History and Culture, part of the federal government's Smithsonian Institution, published a list of cultural attributes they believed represent White culture:

"Individualism, objectivity, rationality, reason, hard work, the nuclear family, a belief in progress, a written tradition, politeness, the justice system, respect for authority, delayed gratification, and planning for the future, among others."

These attributes, which are a recipe for success, are wrongly classified as "aspects and assumptions of Whiteness." This is not White culture. This is American culture, and if internalized by Black people in America, it will deliver success as it does for those who do.

So, virtues like "hard work, being on time, cause and effect, rational thinking, respect for authority, politeness..." are, according to the museum, manifestations of Whiteness?

Can you believe this? These traits are the foundation of any civilized society that functions, no matter what color the citizens are. It's almost as if this list was written by a White supremacist, because the opposite of these traits, would suggest Black people are lazy, can't keep to a schedule, have no respect for authority, can't think straight, are rude, etc.

After national backlash, the museum removed the chart and apologized.

The Museum making the Whiteness list, is just one example of how the progressive left has been able to socially engineer Black society into rejecting cultural principles that are productive. Many Black people have been hoodwinked into embracing a counterfeit culture that has contributed to their own demise.

The Democratic Party policies and progressive ideology have been able to systematically degenerate the Black community over the last fifty years. We see this in the breakdown of the family, the failed Democratic Party–run educational system, and the shifting of culture away from morality and decency. But as I said earlier, every election cycle, the Democratic Party has been able to mask all these deep-rooted issues, convincing the Black community that the biggest issue they face is, racism and racist White cops.

Ultimately, Black Americans as a community must begin to recognize these schemes, and stop aligning themselves with a party whose policies have led to the decline of their communities. If the Black American community is to thrive again, it must rediscover and embrace the values that were at the core of what it truly is. That means going back into history and embracing the cultural values that made them a thriving enduring people who built great communities and invented great things, even in the face of the evils of racial injustice of the time.

CHAPTER 5

DEFINING POSTMODERNISM AND NEO-MARXISM

UNPACKING THE AGENDA
BEHIND RACE AND IDENTITY POLITICS

The boiling frog is an old allegory describing a frog being slowly boiled alive. It goes like this: To boil a frog, you must first place it in a pot with cold water, turn the heat on, and incrementally increase the temperature. As the temperature increases, the frog may feel uncomfortable, but not enough to do anything about it. By the time the water begins to boil, it's too late for the frog to jump out, so the frog boils to death. There would be a different result if you boil the water first. If a frog is suddenly thrown into a pot of hot boiling water, it will immediately leap out. The boiling frog is a perfect metaphor for America.

What we are witnessing in America today is not by happenstance. Division, polarization, identity politics, embrace of socialism, shrinking of the middle-class, cancel culture, and the erosion of the moral fabric of the nation have been socially engineered over time. These things happened as a result of strategic plans that have been incrementally implemented over the last sixty-plus years.

Taking a glimpse into Neo-Marxism and post modernism will shed tremendous light and offer context to what we see taking place in America. Marxism and Communism are alive and well in America. Since the fall of Communism in Eastern Europe, these loser ideologies have been resurrected and reconvened in ways that were more subtle and less obvious, with a more palatable name like Progressivism.

The Progressive movement in America really took root around 1890 to combat what many felt were social ills that plagued society following the industrial revolution. The progressive solution was to give government at the highest levels the power to address these perceived ills as opposed to letting the people and the free market find solutions.

Progressivism is the idea that government should control industry, manage labor unions, manage healthcare, provide transportation, oversee farming, tax the rich, give to the poor, educate our children, and, essentially, dictate to the citizenry how they are supposed to live. The Democratic Party has increasingly taken this position, and it's not by accident.

In his best-selling book *The Naked Communist*, former FBI Special Agent W. Cleon Skousen listed the forty-five Communist/Progressive goals that were listed by American Progressives to overthrow the American ideals. On January 10, 1963, Congressman Albert S. Herlong Jr., of Florida, read a list of forty-five Communist goals into the *Congressional Record*. These were to be carried out over several decades via deception and stealth infiltration, carried out through an influence campaign in all spheres of society, like education, media, and entertainment.

John Eidson, writer for the *Canada Free Press Blog*, summarized Skousen's researched list of objectives as follows:

- Eliminate prayers and any expression of religion in schools

- Infiltrate churches and replace true religion with "social" religion
- Discredit the US Constitution and America's Founding Fathers
- Infiltrate and gain control of the labor union movement
- Infiltrate and gain control of teacher's associations
- Use schools as transmission belts for socialist indoctrination
- Break down traditional cultural standards; discredit the family as an institution
- Infiltrate and gain control of the press, radio, TV, and the entertainment industry
- Use the courts to weaken basic American institutions (like marriage)
- Promote the UN as the only hope for mankind; demand that it be set up as a one-world government
- Infiltrate and gain control of one or both political parties

The Naked Communist details how communists strategically infiltrate an existing political party to achieve their objectives and spread propaganda through information they feed to the seemingly independent media outlets they have infiltrated. Skousen also illustrated how they maneuver their way into society through the youth of a nation with the lure of Socialism, which is the precursor to Communism. The Overton window of what it means to be a free American is increasingly moved further to the left in education, media, and entertainment, until it reaches a point where the youth consider totalitarianism as the norm. Sound familiar?

Skousen's book shocked America and the rest of the free world. It clearly exposed how easily this was being done, while few people were aware of it. It was the first time anyone had defined how people in free capitalist nations are persuaded to choose Communism or Socialism at the expense of their own liberty.

In 1926, when *The Naked Communist* was written some of the book's critics said the author's findings were extreme, because at the time, it seemed improbable. At the time, few Americans realized how much the ideas of Marxism and Communism had infiltrated the nation.

Today, it's easier to see how the list of the Communists' goals detailed in Skousen's book have played out in America. Not only has prayer been taken out of schools but religious expression of any kind in school is now forbidden. America's youth are increasingly embracing Socialism and are sympathetic to Communist ideas. According to a recent YouGov poll, a staggering 70 percent of millennials, people born between 1981 and 1996, said they would be somewhat or extremely likely to vote for a socialist candidate. For a country like America, which was founded on principles of individual liberty and limited government, that is a concerning statistic, to say the least.

It's important to understand that shifts in Americans' attitudes toward socialism didn't happen by accident. As detailed by Skousen, it has been due to a strategic infiltration by Socialists and Communists into the academic system, turning American schools and universities into what I would characterize as Socialist indoctrination camps. These institutions are teaching America's youth that Capitalism is evil, when Capitalism is the only economic system that has been proven to lift people out of poverty, and I can personally testify to that.

Moving along to media and entertainment, we find that these industries are now almost exclusively run and controlled by the progressive left. By gaining control of these spheres of influence since the early 1960s, the progressive left has been able to shape culture and breakdown America's traditional standards to the point that saying something as basic and as truthful as that there are two genders is now a controversial statement.

Now that I have laid this foundation, in order to understand the agenda behind the obsession with race, social justice, and identity politics, it is imperative that we start by briefly describing the ideological roots of these dogmas and how that relates to what's happening in America.

To make sense of this era of hyper-identity politics that we now find ourselves in, you must have a basic understanding of what Postmodernism and neo-Marxism/Communism is. As Christians and Conservatives, these are topics we need to understand in order stand up and counter the encroachment of these dangerous philosophies.

In a video that was not meant for public consumption, one of the founders of the Black Live Matter (BLM) movement clearly states, "We are trained Marxists." The internet exploded at this stunning admission. Of course, many of us who pay attention to their tactics, already knew this was the case. In fact, outspoken conservatives, like Glenn Beck, have been warning us for years. We can now say with confidence that the BLM movement is not a civil rights movement, like the media portrays it to be. Black Lives Matter is a Marxist movement. Why is that so dangerous? What is Marxism?

MARXISM

Marxism is a philosophical, economic, and sociological ideology developed by German philosopher Karl Marx in the late 1800s. Marxism is a political philosophy predicated on class warfare—strife between the haves and the have-nots. According to Marx, society is divided into two classes, the oppressed vs. the oppressor.

The oppressor, also known as the ruling class, is cast as the villain. The villain, according to Marx, "inherits and sustains social legal, and political control, owning the lion's share of the resources." On the other hand, "the oppressed, are in an inescapable condition of poverty and social abuse." The have-nots are to loathe, despise, and deeply resent the haves.

The ultimate quest of Marxism is to change the status quo in order to achieve a more "equitable and just" society. This is to occur by uniting the working class in a violent revolution against the ruling-class. Marxism assumes that when the working class, aka the have-nots, succeed in their revolution to overthrow the ruling class, the working class will relinquish that power and spread it around in a Socialist or Communist utopia, where everyone is equal and shares all the goods and services.

In contrast, Capitalism encourages competition, industriousness, hard work, and laboring to better one's family and community. Marxism sees revolution as the primary way to achieve a Utopian society. The end result is the equal distribution of wealth and labor among all citizens.

The Marxist Revolution's fruits turned out to be quite the opposite. In the twentieth century, Marxism became the leading ideological cause of death, claiming more than a hundred million lives in Europe, Russia, Central and South America, Vietnam, China, etc. In the Soviet Union's Ukraine region, six million people starved to death following a Marxist revolution that fomented resentment by the masses against the farmers, who were the businessmen and producers of the region's food supply.

Historically, Marxism is widely regarded as unsuccessful at achieving more just conditions for the have-nots. By the end of the 1900s, Marxism had such a bad name that academics who still supported it could no longer to do so openly. So it went underground until Marxism found its new home in postmodernism. As my husband would say, it was like putting lipstick on a pig.

POSTMODERNISM

Postmodernism is the philosophy behind the hyper-identity politics. It's the root cause of so much of the strife and bitterness in America today. Defeating this enemy will require a better understanding of the underpinnings of the ideology.

To grasp the concept of what is said to be the postmodern era, let's contrast it with what the modern era is. Helen Pluckrose, author and researcher of the postmodern theory, describes the modern era as follows:

"The modern era is the period of history which saw the Renaissance, Humanism, the Enlightenment, the Scientific Revolution, and the development of liberal values and human rights; the period when Western societies gradually came to value reason and science over faith and superstition as routes to knowledge, and developed a concept of the person as an individual member of the human race deserving of rights and freedoms rather than as part of various collectives subject to rigid hierarchical roles in society."

The *Encyclopedia Britannica* describes postmodernism as "a late 20th-century movement characterized by broad skepticism of grand narratives, subjectivism, or relativism; a general suspicion of reason; and a reaction against the intellectual, philosophical assumptions and values of the modern period of western history."

In short, it's an ideology that essentially says there are no absolutes. For example, there is no single way to explain reality. In postmodernism, there is an unspecified number of interpretations of reality. It rejects objectivity, reason, and intellectual assumptions. It rejects the philosophy that values ethics, reason, clarity, and structure. Embedded in postmodernism is the Marxist ideology of power and oppression. Canadian Professor Jordan Peterson (a *must* follow) explains the relationship between Marxism and postmodernism as follows:

"Where Marxism pits people against one another by economic status, postmodernism, and its offshoot Critical Race Theory, takes it one step further. Postmodernism divides people against one another, based on a number of criteria; i.e. race, religion, gender, sexual orientation, and an ever increasingly smaller subgroups of people. In postmodernism, people are not seen as individuals to be judged on their own merits, but rather as belonging to a collective group."

Unfortunately, postmodernism is increasingly becoming the foundational philosophy. It's not only being taught in universities but has permeated all of society. This toxic philosophy breaks down traditional norms and the elements that create a unified national identity. The balkanization that this poisonous ideology creates is like a cancer, and it could eventually kill this nation. As a nation founded on the principle of freedom, America cannot survive if good men and women don't stand up, speak up, and take action against this destructive ideology.

When you understand this foundation, the destruction of the American structure that we're witnessing begins to make sense. In certain spheres of society, logic, reason, and objectivity are now rejected as relics of a bygone era. For example, I recently found out there is a new television show titled, *My Pregnant Husband*. This program airs on prime-time cable television. I thought this must be a joke, but it's not. It's an actual show. In a postmodern world that rejects the notion of objective reality, men do get pregnant and have periods. This is being promoted by the media, entertainment, and academia.

Several television networks recently aired a bizarre underwear commercial. The ad featured a surreal world where men and boys menstruate. It was an ad for period-proof underwear.

The scene starts with a teenage boy telling his parent, "I think I got my period."

The postmodernist ideology is how we ended up with 102 genders and counting. It's how we ended up with biological males who "feel" like they're women, competing and winning every sport against biological females. As a result, women's sports are now dominated by men who feel like they are women, of course. And somehow, the feminists on the left are okay with this?

In a world where there are no absolutes and everything is relative, anything is possible. According to an article in the *Daily News*, a fifty-two-year old Canadian man left his wife and seven children to live his life as a six-year-old girl. In an emotional video with the gay news site, *The Daily Xtra*, the man says, "I realized I was transgender when I was 46 and since transitioned into a 6 year old girl." In today's postmodern era, this type of bizarre behavior is no longer considered a mental illness. It is strangely considered something to be embraced and celebrated.

I first learned about postmodern theory after stumbling on a series of Jordan Peterson lectures. After watching these brilliant videos, I began to connect the dots. Suddenly, all these seemingly random events happening in the world were not so random. It all started to make sense. I now know why it's impossible to reason with or try to have a civil debate with far-left progressive ideologues. It is because enshrined in their postmodern theology is the idea that discourse and debate are futile. You can't expect to have a reasonable or logical conversation with someone who believes in neither logic nor reason.

Like me, a peer that I grew up with in Zimbabwe also migrated to the United States. Unlike me, she attended school on the East Coast and is now a lawyer. After seven years of higher education, it's no surprise that she is on the left side of the political spectrum.

I just didn't know how far left she was until the topic of transgender came up in one of our private message debates.

For someone on the left, she is open-minded and able to have a civil debate without descending into the usual childish name calling that's all too common from the left. As soon as they start to lose a debate based on facts, they turn to insults. "You're a racist," they say. Or they might say you're a homophobe, a transphobe, or a bigot. These are typical responses to any substantive points made that do not align with their philosophy.

My peer was making the case for transgenderism. I was arguing against it, based on logic, reason, science, and objective reality. We could not even agree on one simple fact—that a man is not a woman.

I asked her point blank, "Can a man be a woman?"

"Well, it depends," she said. "If someone feels like they're a woman, then they indeed are a woman."

I thought, "Wow."

"Gender is just a social construct," she said. She told me she believed that a man who has no female characteristics could decide one day that they're a woman.

She offered a rebuttal to just about every rational point I made about the objective reality based on basic biology. But it was not until I made it personal that she took pause. She then went out of her way to avoid answering my question.

She is an aunt to two beautiful young girls, five and seven years old. I shared a picture of the fifty-two-year-old Canadian man who now lives his life as a six-year-old girl. The man wears a pink tutu with a two pig tails in his hair. He also has a beard. I asked her if she would feel confident leaving her nieces alone with the fifty-two-year-old man, because after all, he was a six-year-old girl. Right?

POSTMODERNISM VS. WESTERN CIVILIZATION

At its core, postmodernism, is a war on reality, as well as on Western Civilization and its founding principles. Western Civilization has birthed the greatest, safest, and most prosperous time in human history. Yes, it also included periods of slavery and colonization. But the latter have always existed, in every civilization.

In his Prager University video, "Why Has the West Been So Successful," Ben Shapiro, editor-in-chief of the *Daily Wire*, and nationally syndicated radio talk show host, lists the unique accomplishments of Western civilization. These accomplishments include "the abolition of slavery, religious tolerance, universal human rights, and the development of the scientific method. Western civilization also gave birth to women's suffrage rights, Civil Rights, lifted billions of people out of poverty, and invented most of the modern world we live in today. Everyone who is alive today, has lived in a world that is almost entirely governed by Western Civilization; from Asia, to Africa, to Europe, and South America."

Ben Shapiro describes the two most important foundational principles of Western Civilization as, the perfect balance between Judeo-Christian values and the Greek method of reason as represented by two ancient cities, Jerusalem and Athens.

He writes, "Jerusalem represents a religious revelation as manifested in the Judeo-Christian tradition: the beliefs that a good God created an ordered universe and that this God demands moral behavior from His paramount creation, man.

The other city, Athens, represents reason and logic as expressed by the great Greek thinkers, such as Plato and Aristotle.

These two ways of thinking—revelation and reason—live in constant tension.

Judeo-Christian religion posits that there are certain fundamental truths handed down to us by a transcendent being. We didn't invent these truths; we received them from God. The rules He lays down for us are vital for building a functioning, moral civilization and for leading a happy life.

Greek thinking posits that we only know truth by what we observe, test, and measure. It's not faith but fact that drives our understanding and exploration of the universe.

Western civilization, and only Western civilization, has found a way to balance religious belief and human reason. Here's how the balance works.

The Judeo-Christian tradition teaches that God created an ordered universe and that we have an obligation to try to make the world better. This offers us purpose and suggests that history moves forward. Most pagan religions taught the opposite: that the universe is illogical and random, and that history is cyclical. History just endlessly repeats itself—in which case, why bother to innovate or create anything new?

Second, Judeo-Christian tradition teaches that every human is created in the image of God. That is, each individual's life is infinitely valuable. This seems self-evident to us now, but only because we have lived with this belief for so long. The far more natural belief is that the strong should subjugate the weak—which is precisely what people did in nearly every society in all of history. Only by recognizing the divine in others did we ever move beyond this amoral thinking toward the concern for human rights, democracy, and free enterprise that characterize the West.

But Judeo-Christian religion alone didn't build our modern civilization. We also required Greek reason to teach us objective observation—that man has the capacity to search beyond revelation for answers.

Greek reason brought us the notion of the natural law, the idea that we could discover the natural purpose—the telos—of everything in creation by looking to its character. Human beings were created with the unique capacity to reason; therefore, our telos was to reason. By investing reason with so much power, Greek thought became integral to the Western mission.

Nowhere is this more perfectly expressed than in the American Revolution, in which the Founding Fathers took the best of the European Enlightenment, with its roots in Greek thought, and the best of Judeo-Christian practice, with its roots in the Bible, and melded them into a whole new political philosophy.

Without Judeo-Christian values, we fall into scientific materialism—the belief that physical matter is the only reality, and therefore also fall into nihilism—the belief that life has no meaning, that we're merely stellar dust in a cold universe.

Without Greek reason, we fall into fanaticism—the belief that fundamentalist adherence to unprovable principles represents the only path toward meaning."

In light of Ben Shapiro's brilliant articulation of Western civilization, you can clearly draw the parallels. Postmodernism is antithetical to these Western ideals. It's essentially at war with logic, reason, and Judeo-Christian values. Is any of this starting to make sense? In the next chapter, let's delve deeper into how postmodernism and neo-Marxism have birthed critical race theory, a philosophy which has become the operating system by which race and identity are weaponized to achieve the political objectives of the progressive left.

CHAPTER 6

UNMASKING CRITICAL RACE THEORY

E ncyclopedia Britannica describes critical race theory as "the view that the law and legal institutions are inherently racist and that race itself, instead of being biologically grounded and natural, is a socially constructed concept that is used by White people to further their economic and political interests at the expense of people of color."

Critical race theory is a branch of the postmodernism tree. Its foundations are based on the Marxian ideas that divide a people into oppressed and oppressor. CRT holds that the White-male-dominated system, which prevails in the Western world, is inherently oppressive to people of other people's race, religion, immigration status, income, sexual orientation, gender etc. Essentially if you're not a White male, you're oppressed, to some degree, and if you're a White male, you're the oppressor by default. It gets more complicated because according to critical race theory, a person can be an oppressor in one way or oppressed in another way. That is where the concept of intersectionality comes in.

INTERSECTIONALITY

Intersectionality, in CRT, is the measure by which a person's level of oppression is determined, based on how many of the demographic identity groups they belong to. For example, a Black man is less oppressed than a Black woman. But a Black woman is less oppressed than a Black lesbian. By the same token, a Black lesbian is less oppressed than a transgender woman, so it goes. As your oppressive categories add up, so do intersectional values. The more categories of oppression someone identifies with, the more moral authority they have. The more victim-statuses a person has, the greater his or her insight and authority to speak on issues related to justice and oppression.

As you can imagine, a straight White male has the least amount of intersectionality in these victim Olympics; therefore, he has the least amount of moral authority. For example, the experience of a gay Black woman is more valuable than the experience of a gay White man. If you're White and are not a part of any oppressed group, surrendering to the oppressed by apologizing for being White, and recognizing your White privilege (aka White guilt), are among some of the prescribed methods of "atonement."

This ideology has become so pervasive and acceptable that even Facebook promoted the sentiments of CRT by installing a "Mute White people" button on their Instagram and Facebook stories during the George Floyd saga.

In summary, CRT is an openly racist ideology that states, all White people are inherently racist and oppressive. This toxic ideology is a cancer that has metastasized in the nation, moving from academia, where it incubated, to almost all spheres of our society. This includes corporations, schools, media, government, and even the military. It is all done under the auspices of promoting diversity and inclusion, and eradicating racism.

CRT is now force fed in mandatory diversity training sessions with students, employees, and corporate executives. In these sessions, White people are often separated from people of other races and taught to accept they are racist, even if they don't believe they are. White people are asked to write apologies to all people of color. It's unbelievable that this cult-like brainwashing is taking place in major cultural institutions.

Christopher Rufo, the editor of *City Journal*, appeared on the Tucker Carlson Tonight show to share the findings of his research into just how pervasive CRT has become in our government. He discovered that it's being taught to all federal bureaucrats and employees, from top to bottom. He said, "Federal employees are being forced to attend 'White privilege' and 'micro aggression' training."

Rufo was able to obtain some of the teaching materials that were used at the training. One such training document included the phrases, "America is a White supremacist nation," and "All White people, regardless of how 'woke' they are, contribute to racism."

Additionally, he discovered that the scientific establishment that creates America's nuclear weapons, had critical race theorists send three of their White executives to a three-day diversity training, or what I would call a three-day re-education camp. They were sent to "deconstruct their White culture." They were subsequently forced to write letters of apologies to all people of color.

This is beyond a cult. It's mind-blowing that this is going on in our nation. It's pure evil. It's the antithesis of Dr. Martin Luther King Jr.'s dream. Dr. King dreamed of "a day when people are not judged by the color of their skin but rather by the content of their character."

PERMANENT RACIAL DIVISION

Just as with Marxism, with CRT there is no remedy to the purported racial divide, except through a revolutionary overthrow of the entire system. It calls for a total restructuring of society, language, and of the very narrative that defines justice by and for those who have been purportedly oppressed.

To the well-meaning, unsuspecting public, CRT is being marketed as a way to promote inclusivity and diversity. For this reason, it has been widely accepted by society. The reality is that this insidious ideology is being used to perpetuate a permanent racial divide. It promotes estrangement rather than friendship, and hostility rather than goodwill among races. Rather than heal the nation by bringing people together based on our national identity as Americans, critical race theory has proven to be poisonous to true community and our common humanity. CRT shares many parallels with old tactics used by the Bolsheviks. It's classic divide and conquer exploitation for political gain.

James Lindsay, an author who has studied CRT, describes eight characteristics and core beliefs of CRT that make it impossible for a nation to ever find racial unity.

"Critical Race Theory:

- Believes racism is present in every aspect of life, every relationship and every interaction and therefore has its advocates look for it everywhere
- Relies on interest convergence (White people only give Black people opportunities and freedoms when it is also in their own interests) and therefore doesn't trust any attempt to make race relations better
- Is against free societies and wants to dismantle them and replace them with something that advocates control

- Only treats race issues as 'Socially constructed groups.' So, there is no individuals in CRT
- Believes science, reason, and evidence are a White way of knowing and that storytelling and lived experience is a Black alternative, which hurts everyone especially Black people
- Rejects all potential alternatives like colorblindness, as forms of racism, making itself the only allowable game in town
- Acts like anyone who disagrees with it must do so for racist and White supremacist reasons, even if those people are Black
- Cannot be satisfied, so it becomes a kind of activist Black hole that threatens to destroy everything it is introduced into"

To summarize these points, it is clear that there is no winning or solutions with CRT. Over time, it leads to violence and permanent division. The breakdown of civil discourse and the violence we're seeing in our streets are the fruits of decades of CRT indoctrination that has seeped through from our education system, media, and entertainment.

How can anyone expect anything else out of an ideology that demonizes one race as the source of all evil and all that plagues minority communities? Isn't that all too similar to what Hitler did? If you were to replace the word *White* with the word *Jew* in the training materials of critical race theory, it would sound like the Nazis' manual on hatred of Jews. So why has it become socially acceptable to demonize White people collectively as a race?

In September of 2020, President Trump wrote an executive order banning the teaching of CRT and sensitivity training in government agencies. He tweeted: "A few weeks ago, I BANNED efforts to indoctrinate government employees with divisive and harmful sex and race-based ideologies...." In a second post he said, "Today, I've expanded that ban to people and companies that do business with our Country, the United States Military, Government Contractors, and Grantees. Americans should be taught to take PRIDE in our Great Country, and if you don't, there's nothing in it for you!"

This directive is a clear affirmation of Dr. Martin Luther King Jr.'s vision of an America in which people are "not judged by the color of their skin but by the content of their character." President Trump went on to call CRT "a sickness that cannot be allowed to continue." That was a bold and necessary stand for the vision of racial unity promoted by Dr. King and against the left's revisionist narrative about America.

THE TRUTH ABOUT RACISM

Racism is a sin. It has always existed and always will. Since the fall of mankind in the garden of Eden, has there ever been a sin that has been eradicated? None. Not one. So why does the left set this unattainable goal of eradicating racism? Have you noticed that many of the progressive left's goals are usually an unattainable utopian fantasy?

And according to them, everyone has to live in misery unless that unattainable goal is achieved.

It doesn't have to be that way. Race and racism don't have to be a part of your life. I don't need everyone to like me to live a good and fruitful life, neither does anyone else. If someone doesn't like me because of my skin color (and I'm sure there are some out there that don't), it has nothing to do with me and does not affect my life in anyway. If it does affect my life, there is legal recourse I can take if need be.

Under critical race theory, the progressive left has had to change and broaden the definition of racism in order to fulfil their political objectives.

According to the *Oxford Dictionary*, racism is defined as, "Prejudice, discrimination, or antagonism directed against a person or people on the basis of their membership in a particular racial or ethnic group. Also: The belief that different races possess distinct characteristics, abilities, or qualities, especially so as to distinguish them as inferior or superior to one another."

This is what we have known to be the definition of racism. Under this definition, anyone of any race is capable of racism. However according to CRT, only White people can be racist, so the progressive left set about to have the definition of racism changed and broadened to fit the CRT narrative. They have succeeded to the point that dictionaries are changing the definition of what it means to be racist.

Following a complaint by Kennedy Mitchum, a twenty-two-year-old recent graduate of Drake University, *Merriam Webster's Dictionary* updated its definition of the word *racism*. Mitchum claimed the definition was too simple and was being used to dismiss broader issues of "racial inequality and systemic oppression."

Over several months following the George Floyd incident, the commonly used definition of racism has radically changed in mainstream society. A wave of progressive scholars, activists, and pundits—with the explicit intent to expand the concept of racism—have gained a footing in mainstream media and culture. Among these is celebrated progressive author and historian Ibram Kendi, who's central intellectual contribution has been to redefine racism.

In his book *How to Be an Antiracist*, he argues there is no such thing as "not racist," there is only antiracist and racist. According to Kendi, claiming not to be racist is denial and is itself the "heartbeat of racism." For Kendi, antiracism means supporting and instituting policies and ideas that level racial disparities of socio-economic outcome, while racism is defined as any system, policy, or idea that results in racial inequality.

In essence, we're seeing a redefining of racism as any system or institution that does not produce equal outcomes among all races. Once again, the idea of producing equal outcomes is an unattainable utopian fantasy. So by this measure, progressives accuse America of being a racist and systemically oppressive nation. America has never promised equal outcomes. What America does promise is equal opportunity. The outcomes for everyone will vary depending on to what extent a person takes advantage of those opportunities, along with other variables.

By this new definition of racism, anyone who is seen to not actively support the institution of policies that produce equal outcomes among all races, is racist. That means if you do not believe in the Communist ideals of equal outcomes but believe in equal opportunity, congratulations, you are a "racist." This definitional shift of racism flows naturally from the underlying progressive assumption that all racial disparities are always a consequence of racism, which I have demonstrated in previous chapters to be a false assertion.

CRT itself is the textbook definition of racism and should be rejected in all its forms. Its false assertion that only White people are capable of the evil that is racism is a denial of reality. In my own personal life, I have encountered racist people of all races, including racist Black people. It is human nature for people to like and want to be around people who look like them.

Our primal instinct is to like and want to be around people who are like us not just racially, but in other ways too. Human beings are tribal by nature. You know the cliche, "Birds of a feather flock together." Its true.

THE TRUTH ABOUT PREJUDICE

Every human being, including me, has some form of racial prejudice. Prejudice just means that we prejudge others. If you claim to not prejudge people, situations, circumstance, then you're not being honest with yourself. Prejudice is a survival instinct that's built into every human being and is not limited to just race. We form prejudices based on experiences and stereotypes we perceive about a racial group.

Jason Riley, Black researcher, and author of the book *Please Stop Helping Us*, artfully describes what prejudice looks like. He describes a Black federal judge named Theodore McKee as having said the following during an interview with another Black judge:

"Some individuals who avoid encounters with Black youths may indeed be acting out of racism. But given that law abiding Black youth exhibit the same exact behaviors, it is likely that most people are acting on probability. If I am walking down the road in Center City Philadelphia at 2:00 a.m. in the morning, and I hear some footsteps behind me and I turn around and there a couple of young White dudes behind me, I am probably not going to get very uptight. I am probably not going to have the same reaction as if I turn around and there is the proverbial Black urban youth behind me.... Now if I can have this reaction, and I am a Black male who has studied martial arts for twenty some odd years and can defend myself, I can't help but think that the average White judge in the situation, will have a reaction that is ten times more intense."

Perceptions and stereotypes of Black criminality are based on the reality of high Black crime rates. The progressive left glosses over this fact, blaming racism every time. Anything to shift the responsibility away from themselves. According to critical race theory, the more oppressed identity groups an individual belongs to, the less moral responsibility they have for their actions.

Therefore because (per CRT) Black people are oppressed, the conversation about why the racial stereotypes of Black criminality persist, is rendered irrelevant. It must just be because people are racist, the left claims.

Don't be so naïve as to the think the reason why the masterminds of the progressive left traffic in this racism narrative is for any other reason than a self-serving one. The incentive to keep the racism narrative alive is not only politically but monetarily expedient.

Jason Riley, writes about this industry created around racism that is exploited by modern-day, so called Black civil rights leaders:

"The Black civil rights leadership is fully aware that Black criminality is at its root, a Black problem that needs to be addressed by Black people, reassessing Black behavior and cultural attitudes. But the Civil Rights Movement has become an industry and that industry has no vested interest in realistic assessment."

Race has been weaponized by the left as tool to gain power and raise billions of dollars that barely benefit the average Black person. It's a system of control and fundraising that works well for them. Even though great civil rights strides have been achieved since the 1960s, it's financially crucial for these groups that the perception of systemic racism be kept alive, while real issues that plague Black communities, like crime and violence, are swept under the rug.

TRIBALISM, RACISM, AND SLAVERY

In Africa, tribalism is a real thing. You can have two African tribes that you can't physically tell apart, and they can be at war with each other. For example, a large number of Black South Africans don't like Zimbabweans who migrated to South Africa for opportunity. Black South Africans even have racial slurs for

Zimbabweans like me. As an American, you may not be able to tell a Zimbabwean and a South African apart, but we, as Africans, can tell each other apart. The animosity toward Zimbabweans in South Africa is so bad that some Zimbabweans live in fear for their lives. Xenophobic hate crimes against Zimbabweans are commonplace.

Even within Zimbabwe, there are tensions that go back centuries between the Ndebele tribe, a minority tribe in south of Zimbabwe, and the Shona tribe in the north, of which I am a part. The majority Shona are the dominant tribe. Therefore, they dominate the hierarchical structure of the nation.

As sure as the sun will rise tomorrow morning, human beings are always going to gravitate toward tribalism. This tribalism can transcend race and can be based on hierarchy or ideology.

So, this notion that White people have a monopoly on the evils that are racism, prejudice, and even slavery, is a narrow-minded worldview. These are afflictions that have been suffered by the entire human race, all over the planet. But for critical race theorists, whose clear agenda is to undermine Western civilization, it's imperative that slavery is viewed only through the narrow lens of Europeans enslaving Africans. In doing so, CRT undermines and understates an evil that has plagued mankind since the beginning of time.

The idea behind the postmodern critical race theory is to portray slavery as a peculiarly American or peculiarly White crime. Unfortunately, this manipulation has been successful. When one conjures up images around the word *slavery*, the images that immediately come to mind are those of Europeans enslaving and whipping Africans in the, fifteenth and sixteenth centuries.

While America's history of slavery is conjured up to a high degree in pop culture, academia, media, and entertainment, the modern-day traumas of slavery, which still exists in parts of Africa and the Middle East, go unnoticed. The wider history of slavery that is seen throughout all cultures has also been ignored.

Black American conservative intellectual Thomas Sowell documents a more comprehensive history of slavery in his book: *Black Rednecks and White Liberals*. In his book, he reveals:

A large number of African slaves were traded by Islamic slave traders from the Middle East and North Africa. Europeans were also captured and enslaved at the hands of Arab Muslims for centuries.

Between 1500–1800 A.D., at least 1 million White European slaves were enslaved by North African pirates. Some European slaves, were still being sold on the auction blocks, years after slavery had ended for blacks in America. On August 4, 1877, an Anglo-Egyptian treaty ended the sale of White slaves in Egypt. Eastern European Slavs, were widely captured as slaves, in both Europe and the Islamic world. So much so, that the word *slave* was derived from the word *Slav*, describing Eastern Europeans from the Slavic nations.

Asians also have a long history of slavery. China and India are both well-known to have had the largest, most comprehensive markets for the exchange of human beings, having more slaves than all of the western hemisphere.

You wonder why this broader context of the history of slavery is not being taught or discussed? The answer to this question lies in the fact, that the true history of slavery, does not fit into a narrow perception. The falsehood that it is only Whites who are capable of the evils of slavery.

The fruit of this pervasive CRT indoctrination is that it creates resentment toward Whites—"the haves." This resentment is kin to the Marxist ideology that was designed to create resentment for the rich producers. As a result, hate crimes against Whites have increased exponentially. They receive little to media coverage. The hatred this ideology creates toward White people is just as ugly as the hatred the KKK has toward Black people.

In Kansas City, Missouri, two Black teens recently attacked a thirteen-year-old White boy on his front porch as he was returning from school. They poured gasoline on him and set him on fire for no apparent reason, shouting, "You get what you deserve, White boy!" Note that this story did not make the national news. Had the race of the individuals involved been reversed, it would have been an explosive national story. The reason is because the story, as it stands, does not fit the racial narrative they want portrayed.

Between 2012 and 2015, Blacks committed 85.5 percent of all interracial violent crime (including interracial homicide, which is also disproportionately Black-on-White). The stories surrounding this statistic are largely ignored by the media. At the same time, the less frequent White on Black crime is extensively covered and promoted by the media.

For most people, these facts are uncomfortable to talk about. People are too afraid to be called racist for stating the reality that contradicts the false narrative that Americans are being force-fed daily. Indeed, you will most likely be called a racist, as I have been called a "race traitor" and "Uncle Tom," for speaking up and countering the progressive left's narrative. Name calling is a tactic the left uses to shut down debate. Sadly, it works for them. They silence the voices of many who are now deterred from speaking for fear of being smeared, berated, suspended, shadow banned, fired, or "cancelled."

If we live in a society where facts matter, then Black Lives Matter's protests and riots would have never happened. The movement is nakedly predicated on the lie that it is Black people whose lives are in danger from White people. Sadly, we know the protests will continue, and the media and Hollywood will continue to cheer them on.

Objective truth and reality apparently do not have a place in the conversation. In fact, the left does not want to have a truthful conversation about this topic. The only thing that matters to the progressive power structure is the political power that is derived from racially divisive ideologies and movements like CRT and Black Lives Matter. These are harmful not only to the country but are even more harmful to the Black community the progressive left purports to represent.

CHAPTER 7

THE HIDDEN AGENDA BEHIND BLACK LIVES MATTER (BLM)

"Cops kill two times as many Whites as Blacks. Cops kill at least as many unarmed Whites as unarmed blacks. In the USA, half of homicide victims are Black, almost all killed by Blacks. The number one cause of preventable death for White males: accidents. The number one cause of death for Black males: homicide by Blacks."

— Larry Elder

Following the death of George Floyd, a Black man, allegedly at the hands of a White police officer, the entire nation was rocked to its core. The sheer magnitude of what was reported as a heinous hate crime was unacceptable to millions of Americans, including myself, across all political spectrums.

In the reported story, police officers had been called to a crime scene after George Floyd allegedly tried to pass a counterfeit twenty-dollar bill to buy cigarettes at a convenience store. When the police arrived to answer the call, according to a later released video, Mr. Floyd was arrested and placed in the back of a police car, where he said, "I can't breathe." He continued to resist arrest and ultimately found himself on the street with an officer's knee on the back of his neck. He repeatedly told the officer, "I can't breathe." After eight minutes, Floyd appeared to stop breathing. He subsequently died. It was heartbreaking to watch.

The immediate media narrative was that a racist, White police officer purposefully and callously murdered a Black man in broad daylight.

For a brief moment in time, the entire country seemed united in one chorus, condemning the actions of the police officer. Political leaders and pundits from both sides of the aisle called for the officer's arrest. Within four days, the officer was arrested and charged with second- and third-degree murder.

But the prompt arrest and charging the officer with murder did not deter the progressive left from capitalizing on the incident. They were quick to seize on the opportunity to perpetuate months of 24/7 sensationalized media coverage. The goal was clear: create as much racial division within the country as possible. This incident was just what the left needed to prove, once and for all, that America was indeed a systemically racist, White supremacist country.

Is that really the conclusion we're supposed to come to following this tragic incident? It's not, if you know the truth that would give what transpired the proper context. Although one tragic death is one too many, incidents of unarmed Black men killed by White police officers are statistically rare. However, the progressive media portrays these incidents as rampant and commonplace in today's America.

Irresponsible far left progressive activists, masquerading as journalists, even go so far as to suggest that Black people are routinely being hunted down and murdered by the police. Out of the 63 million encounters law enforcement has with US citizens each year, fewer than a dozen unarmed Black men are killed, on average, by the police. The number of unarmed White men killed by police is higher than that of Blacks both in number and by percentage as it relates to crimes committed. It is also important to note, 'unarmed' does not mean they did not pose imminent danger to the police officer in most of the cases.

The truth is police shootings are occurring more frequently in areas where police officers confront armed or violently resisting suspects. Those suspects are disproportionately Black. According to the most recent study by the Department of Justice, although Blacks were only 15 percent of the population in the seventy-five largest counties in the U.S., they were charged with 62 percent of all robberies, 57 percent of murders, and 45 percent of assaults. In New York City, Blacks commit over 75 percent of all shootings, though they are only 25 percent of the city's population. Whites on the other hand, commit only 2 percent of all shootings, though they are 34 percent of the population.

These numbers help provide us with the proper context as to what is driving the statistics on police shootings. It is the unpopular truth, the elephant in the room no one wants to talk about. Black people are disproportionately committing more crimes and as a result, they have more police encounters. Wouldn't it be judicious to address this issue at its root and ask why crime rates are so high in the black community, and then work towards solving this major issue? It would make more sense for sure but as I have come to find out, it is not really about solving real issues, it's about getting people to react emotionally for political gain.

Emotion always trumps facts and statistics. The progressive left knows this and has therefore mastered this art of deception. Getting people to react emotionally and not rationally is an extremely effective strategy for them.

BLACK LIVES MATTER INC.

The vast majority of Americans in 2020 agree with the sentiment that Black lives do matter. And therein lies the brilliance and genius of BLM's name and marketing slogan. If you don't support an organization with a name that declares that Black lives matter, then that means you don't believe Black lives matter. This automatically makes you a racist. Who wants to be labeled racist? Nobody. This is the shield behind which the organization hides behind from any scrutiny or criticism.

What and who is behind Black lives matter? What are their objectives? It's not what most people have been led to believe by popular culture.

From the onset, BLM's primary claims have been completely unfounded. The false narrative—that the organization propagates with the help of the media—is a dangerous myth. Factually, police officers are *not* systematically targeting and hunting down Black Americans to be killed. Police officers are not motivated by systemic, overt racism, or implicit racial bias, to callously kill Black people in cold blood as claimed by BLM. The death of George Floyd and other Black men, at the hands of police, is not proof of a broader systemic racism within American law enforcement. These mendacious claims are unsupported by the facts and statistical data, which we will get into. But who cares about the facts, when facts, logic, and reason are apparently tools of White supremacy?

We have all witnessed the civil unrest in the nation, sparked by the death of George Floyd and other Black individuals. My goal for this chapter is to help Americans make sense of what they have seen take place in the nation with regard to race. Specifically, I want Christians and conservatives to understand the truth about Black Lives Matter, Inc. It is important that we know the truth about the claims they make, their stated objectives, and their true agenda.

I've seen a lot of well-meaning Christians touting the BLM mantra on social media, without knowing what exactly they're supporting and coming into agreement with. They agree with the sentiment that Black lives matter as any Christian should, but most don't understand the organization and the ideology behind that seemingly innocuous phrase. The church should be educated and lead on these issues, instead of sheepishly following the world in supporting a movement that is clearly hostile to the Gospel.

The Black Lives Matter movement was never really popular or accepted in mainstream America in the past (for reasons that will become obvious later in this chapter). Post George Floyd, suddenly it was embraced by just about everyone. Corporations big and small championed the cause. Churches, friends, and neighbors were all too quick to jump on the hysterical bandwagon. The left did not let this crisis go to waste. The narrative in the nation quickly became that White people were collectively guilty for the actions of this one White police officer. By the same token, all black people were collectively victims, vicariously through George Floyd.

It all quickly devolved into an apparent collective nervous breakdown. In acts of virtue and self-flagellation, many White Americans concluded that Floyd's death somehow confirmed their own racism, which they needed to exorcise. In what looked like religious rituals, White people were seen on bended knees, kissing feet, apologizing to Blacks for being White.

It became apparent that the only way a White person in 2020 would be allowed in polite society, the only way they would be perceived as decent, was if they accepted culpability for Floyd's death and the systemically racist society they apparently helped create.

White people now had to apologize for their privilege and internalize and come to grips with their supposed unconscious, deep-seated racism.

On June 2, 2020, Instagram was flooded with pictures of black boxes in support of Black Lives Matter activists. My Instagram feed turned Black. Almost everyone I knew was participating. Even Friends and family members, who I have known to be aware of the left's devices, were all onboard with this exercise. The herd mentality fueled by peer pressure was stunning.

It was one of those days that I thought to myself, "I know too much." I know the true nature of the agenda behind BLM that most people may not be aware of or would care to find out. I know who funds the organization and why. I know the premise the movement is built upon is false. Black people are not being hunted down and killed by White people. This is just not the case. I know BLM does nothing to better the lives of the Black communities. Most of the money they raise ends up in the pockets of mostly White Democratic politicians and far left organizations. So, you can imagine my frustration as I watched in astonishment. Millions of people on social media feeling good about themselves in a futile exercise.

I spoke privately with some friends and family to see where their heads were. The consensus was that they felt the peer pressure to participate. They had to prove they were not racist. I even had one friend tell me she had to embrace Black Lives Matter daily on social media, lest she endure accusations of racism at her workplace.

I was shocked and deeply grieved at how, seemingly overnight, this toxic ideology I had seen mostly exposed on YouTube videos of happenings at universities, had quickly taken root in the mainstream culture. These are ideas that would have never been contemplated just a few years ago, let alone tolerated in America's fabric. Even the church was embracing all of this.

Suddenly, I found myself in a world where even my pastor and his wife, who had never dared to express any political opinion, on any issue, were now pretty much acknowledging *their* ostensible White privilege. They even posted Black Lives Matter slogans on the church's social media pages and the building itself.

My pastor wasn't the only one jumping on the BLM band-wagon. Many of the prominent church leaders I respected were going all in. I can understand the world embracing this, but to see members of the body of Christ embrace this notion of collective guilt based on one's skin color really grieved my spirit. I had three weeks of sleepless nights.

It became clear to me that most Christians were completely unaware of what BLM stood for and what their objectives were. Black Lives Matter stated this as one of their objectives on their website: "We disrupt the Western-prescribed nuclear family struc-ture requirement by supporting each other as extended families."

Another BLM objective I found on their website was this: "We foster a queer-affirming network. When we gather, we do so with the intention of freeing ourselves from the tight grip of heteronor-mative thinking, or rather, the belief that all in the world are het-erosexual (unless s/he or they disclose otherwise)."

Simply put, BLM's goal is to dismantle the nuclear family structure which is the foundation of civil society. They also intend to dismantle the idea that heterosexuality is the norm in society and replace it with a society that sees LGBTQ+ as the norm.

Ryan Bomberger, a Black American Christian activist, founded the Radiance Foundation. On his blog, he gave ten reasons why he, as a Christian, does not support the BLM movement. In his blog post, he implores Christians to take heed of this sinister orga-nization. Among the reasons is the fact that the organization has no goal of forgiveness and reconciliation. This goes against the basic tenets of the Christian faith. It is a movement of vengeance, anger, and bitterness, the antithesis to Dr. Martin Luther King Jr.'s message and approach.

Dr. King said, "In the process of gaining our rightful place, we must not be guilty of wrongful deeds. Let us not seek to satisfy our thirst for freedom by drinking from the cup of bitterness and hatred. We must forever conduct our struggle on the high plane of dignity and discipline."

Another of Bomberger's reasons for not supporting BLM is the movement's emphasis on "Black power." This concept contradicts Dr. Martin Luther King Jr., who promoted "God's Power and human power." Any movement that purports racial dominance is not of God. The movement's founders openly express hatred of White people. BLM co-founder Toronto Yusra Khogali wrote in a 2016 Facebook post, "White people are a genetic defect of Blackness…Whiteness is not humanness." In another Facebook post, Khogali wrote, "In fact, White skin is sub-human."

Another notable difference between BLM and the King-led movement is the sentiment held toward America. BLM is scornful of America. The country is cast as a fundamentally flawed and racially unjust nation whose sins can't be atoned for. So, the only thing that must be done, is to tear-down and burn the entire system so they can rebuild their new nirvana.

Dr. Martin Luther King Jr. had a different approach that is unifying. His message resonated with Americans of all races because it held America's heritage and ideals in high esteem. Dr. Martin Luther King Jr. did not tear down America with his words. He did not tear down America with his hands. Instead, he called on America to live up to its great ideals.

Black Lives Matter is a movement that is at odds with everything the Christian faith stands for. This movement singles out one race, the White race, as one that is collectively guilty of the sin of racism. The implication is that other races don't have any collective sins to be guilty of. The Bible says, ALL mankind is evil and fallen in our nature. Thus, White people are no more guilty or fallen than any other race of people.

> "All we like sheep have gone astray; we have turned—everyone—to his own way; and the LORD has laid on him the iniquity of us all.", – (Isaiah 53:6, KJV)

Ultimately, we are accountable for our own individual sins. The idea of the collective guilt of an entire race of people based on the bad actions of a few is not biblical.

SHORT HISTORY OF BLM

Conservative author and former left-wing ideologue David Horowitz, in a lengthy and well-documented piece, wrote this brief summary of the BLM movement, including its origins:

> Black Lives Matter emerged as a national presence in the years 2014 and 2015 by declaring war on America's law enforcement agencies. Black Lives Matter activists made headlines occupying America's streets, targeting racially integrated and even majority minority police forces whom they accused of killing blacks at random, merely because they were Black. The Black Lives Matter activists fomented riots, burned and looted cities, and incited their followers with chants that ranged from "What do we want? Dead Cops! When do we

want them? Now!" to "Hands Up, Don't Shoot...."
Black Lives Matter was formed in 2013 by three
self-styled "Marxist-Leninist revolutionaries,"
who selected as their movement icon convicted
cop-killer and Black Liberation Army member
Assata Shakur.

Shakur had fled to Cuba, after being convicted
of the homicide she committed when her car was
stopped for a broken taillight by two New Jersey
state troopers. Without any warning, Shakur shot
trooper Werner Foerster. The 34-year-old Vietnam
veteran was lying wounded on the ground pleading
for his life, when Shakur walked over and executed
him. Officer Foerster left a widow and a three-
year-old son.

Black Lives Matter activists refer to the murderer
as "our beloved Assata Shakur" and chant her
words as a ritual, "at every meeting, every event,
every action, every freeway we've shut down,
every mall we've shut down." The chant is this:
"It is our duty to fight for our freedom. It is our duty
to win. We must love and support one another. We
have nothing to lose but our chains."

The last line is lifted directly from the conclusion
to the Communist Manifesto, a document and war
cry that has led to the murders of millions.

Black Lives Matter was at the center of a
very large network, including hundreds of leftist
organizations sharing the same vision. Many
of these organizations are funded by America's
largest corporations and philanthropies, including
the Ben & Jerry Foundation, the Ford Foundation,

the Rockefeller Foundation, the Margaret Casey Foundation, the Nathan Cummings Foundation, and George Soros's Open Society Institute.

In the summer of 2016, the Ford Foundation and Borealis Philanthropy announced the formation of the Black-Led Movement Fund, a six-year pooled donor campaign whose goal was to raise $100 million for the Movement for Black Lives coalition. This coalition embodies the extremist views and agendas of the Black Lives Matter radicals.

To summarize, BLM is a Communist Marxist organization founded by three lesbian Leninists and funded by White left wing billionaires.

BLM—FOLLOW THE MONEY

With Marxism, power is the only goal. So, you should not be surprised to learn that BLM does little, if anything, to contribute to solving the real systemic issues in the Black community. In 2020 alone, BLM "protesters" have destroyed over 2.2 billion dollars in property. Much of the damage was to Black owned businesses in distressed communities.

Black Lives Matter has mastered the art of hiding behind their propaganda and their claim of wanted social justice and equality for Black people. They go so far as to present themselves as a civil rights movement, when, in reality, they're a Marxist movement. Their goal is overthrowing the social, cultural, political, and economic system of America. This can be seen by the organization's lack of involvement in the areas that truly affect Black lives, like education, economic empowerment, crime, and violence in Black communities. BLM has fundraised over ten billion dollars;

however, very little to none of that money ever makes its way into the hands of the Black communities they purport to represent.

Even the left-wing organization FactCheck.org admits that a total of "71% of the money donated to Black Lives Matter goes to salaries, benefits, and consulting fees." The money donated is also funneled to Act Blue, the activist arm of the Democratic Party.

This organization takes 3.9 percent of every donation, and if donations are unclaimed in sixty days, 100 percent of the money goes into Act Blue's funds, which is then doled out to various left-wing activist organizations.

Some of the organizations receiving this money include:

- The Bail Project—helps pay bail for protestors.
- Reclaim the block—works with communities and city council members to defund the police and redistribute the funds elsewhere.
- The Okra Project—pays Black trans chefs to go into the homes of Black trans people to cook them meals at no cost.

It's clear Black Lives Matter is more concerned with pushing far left objectives. Among them, transgenderism, the war on the nuclear family, and even abortion on demand. BLM is a well-funded, left-wing organization that works tirelessly to fundamentally transform America.

BLM "PROTESTS," RIOTING, AND LOOTING

Following the George Floyd incident, we saw massive protests erupt across the country, and even around the world. As I write this book, we are witnessing this civil unrest continue.

Initially, many well-meaning Americans took to the streets because they felt moved to stand up against what they saw as a gross injustice. The initial images of a police officer kneeling on neck of George Floyd's neck as be cried "I can't breathe" were horrific to watch. The media played the video at the top of every hour, twenty-four hours a day for what might have been weeks.

It didn't take long before what started out as organic peaceful protests turned violent and unruly. Antifa, a far-left group of mostly millennial White men and women, recently designated a domestic terror group, showed up in many cities across the nation. They hit the streets and allied their organization with the BLM professionally organized protestors. These are well funded organizations and are by no-means organic, as portrayed by the media.

We saw businesses, stores, buildings, communities, even churches, destroyed and burned to ashes in many cities across the country. We witnessed the looting of Target stores and even high-end stores in affluent neighborhoods.

A heartbreaking video of a Black business owner weeping after his business was looted and destroyed went viral on social media. He told a reporter that he had, spent his entire life savings for this sports bar, that now lay in ruins. Tragically, he had no property insurance to cover the damage done to his property. Thankfully, a group of conservative activists started a GoFundMe page for him, and they successfully raised $60,000 for him to help restore his business.

But he was not alone. Many videos, of mostly Black Americans grieving at the destruction of their communities went viral on social media. The videos received little to no coverage by the media networks. Instead, the media tacitly promoted the riots and the destruction of property as justified, because "America is racist." Chris Cuomo, of CNN even said, "This violence was not only justified but was a constitutional right."

We watched as Hollywood celebrities and athletes, from the comfort of their gated communities, with private security, encouraged Black people to destroy their own communities. These celebrities were promising to pay their bail if arrested, and they did.

Chrissy Teigen tweeted, "I am committed to donating $100,000 to the bail-outs of protestors across the country." Numerous celebrities, like Cynthia Nixon, of *Sex and the City*, tweeted they would match it.

Joe Biden's staff members, and vice-presidential nominee Kamala Harris, also tweeted out support for the rioters. They even posted links for donations to a fund that would provide the money needed to bail-out anyone arrested for destruction of property or violence. This all was shocking to me. How did America come to this? Is America now a place where the destruction of the private property of innocent Americans is celebrated?

Protests, riots, looting, and destruction of property continues even now, as I write this book. LA is in flames, due to reports of another shooting of an unarmed Black man by police. Portland is now on day ninety of riots and destruction. Who is behind all this? How can protests be sustained for this long without organization and funding.

What's happening is by no means organic. Police departments across the nation continue to report that the majority of people arrested in the riots are from out of town. Many of them are professional rioters that are being paid and bussed in or flown to cities across the country, just to cause maximum damage.

According to a news report from The Hill, Kenosha police said, "The majority of the people they arrested for rioting and destruction of property, were from 44 different cities across the country. Of the 175 arrests, 102 listed addresses that were from outside of Kenosha, Wisconsin. It was reported that arrest numbers included people from 44 different cities." Clearly, these were not organic protests. Someone is funding the anarchy, but who?

At the height of the George Floyd riots, some telling videos surfaced. In them, Black Americans, who had come to protest peacefully, questioned how and why pallets of bricks mysteriously appeared on city streets. The bricks were strategically placed right in front of a building with large windows. One video that was shared multiple times shows a car with two young people. The car stops, and the White couple in the car attempts to hand a Black couple some bricks. The Black woman accosts the White couple, for assuming that because she was Black, she was part of the effort to riot and loot.

Another video, widely shared on social media, features two White Antifa women spraying graffiti on a Starbucks building. A Black woman appears and pleads with them to stop. She says, "This is not what we want. Please don't destroy our community. We just want to peacefully protest." But the White women ignore her and continue to vandalize.

Many of the leaders of BLM have defended the riots stating that they were justified.

Ariel Atkins, a BLM activist in Chicago, said at a rally, "I don't care if someone decides to loot a Gucci or a Macy's or a Nike store, because that makes sure that person eats, that makes sure that person has clothes." She goes on to say, "Looting is reparations."

The leader for BLM New York defended the looting and rioting saying, "America is a terrorist country that steals and pillages different countries!"

To date, the BLM protests have caused more than an estimated one billion dollars in property damage, much of which was perpetrated in Black communities. As I write this book, BLM riots have also claimed the lives of forty-eight people, most of them Black. Ironically, the BLM protests, in just a few short months, have cost more Black lives than the number of Black lives lost to police in the last two years.

The economic fallout from this destruction is something that receives extraordinarily little media attention, if any. Businesses are now forced to flee many of these neighborhoods destroyed by the BLM and Antifa riots. As the businesses go, so go the jobs and opportunities for the people in those communities. The loss of jobs has been devastating. Many depend on these jobs to make a living and feed their families.

Another devastating consequence of the destruction is that it adversely effects the elderly, who depend on the walkable proximity of these stores to their homes. An elderly Minneapolis Black woman was interviewed as she mourned the destruction of her community. She recounted how afraid she was the night of the riots. She told the reporter that she used to walk to the grocery store that was now a pile of ash. She continued to say she was now forced to take a bus to the other side of town to get her groceries."

The riots also caused a drop in property values for the Black homeowners in their communities. As businesses leave, commercial property is boarded up and left desolate. The values of the homes in those areas plunge. The void left behind by the lack of jobs and opportunity is filled by hopelessness that leads to alcoholism and drug use. Soon, gangs take ground, and violence is on the rise.

So, what has BLM accomplished for Black people and their communities, from all the protesting, rioting, and looting? Nothing, at best! At worst, they have cost the lives and livelihoods of many Black lives that they purport to stand for. They bring devastation to once thriving neighborhoods. Which leads me to ask if Black lives really do matter to those who are at the forefront of this organization. Clearly not.

ALL BLACK LIVES MATTER

If BLM is 100 percent successful in fulfilling their objective, and the number of deaths of Black men at the hands of police goes down to zero, then BLM would have saved a fraction of a percentage of Black lives lost to killings.

The BLM movement, and their democratic allies, are selective about what Black lives do matter and what Black lives do not. According to BLM, the small percentage of Black lives, taken at the hands of police, or White people, are the ones that matter and deserve amplification.

BLACK-ON-BLACK CRIME

The mere mention of the staggering statistics for Black-on-Black murders is always a trigger to the progressive left. The retort is always, "What about White-on-White crime? What about Hispanic-on-Hispanic crime?" And so on. The answer is that Black-on-Black crime is a serious problem that is unique to the Black community in that it is the number one killer of Black men ages fifteen to forty-four.

According to CDC data compiled in 2011, out of all causes of death, homicide claimed the most Black lives between ages of fifteen and thirty-four years. This was significantly higher than the national average for males of that age group in all other racial groups. The number one killer for Hispanic and White men ages fifteen to thirty-four is not homicide. According to the same CDC data, the number one killer for non-Black males in this age group is unintentional injuries or accidents.

Black-on-Black crime does not fit the BLM narrative. One glaring example of this happened when Black retired police officer David Dorn was murdered by BLM looters in Saint Louis,

Missouri. He was responding to a friend's pawn shop's security alarm when he was shot to death. All the while, the horrific crime was live streamed on Facebook. The Black life of this upstanding man received no media coverage, and the left showed no concern for the tragic killing of Officer Dorn. Why? Apparently because it is a Black life that can't be exploited for their political ends.

Black people are killing each other at alarming rates. Black Lives Matter is not concerned with the nearly seven thousand Black men, women, and children's lives lost to homicide by other Black people in 2019 alone.

As BLM protests rage across the country, Black-on-Black crime and murders have surged dramatically. Chicago, which is already a hotbed for gang violence, has seen an exponential increase in shootings in Black neighborhoods. In the month of June 2020, Chicago saw their deadliest weekend, with over 104 people shot, fourteen died, including a three-year-old boy and multiple teenagers.

It's important to note that these horrific, violent acts are being perpetrated on Black Americans by other Blacks. Yet, this continues to be the big elephant in the room that we are not allowed to discuss. If Black lives matter, then why would the organization that stands for Black lives not acknowledge that which is responsible for the vast majority of lives lost to killings?

The tragedy is that the majority of the homicide cases go unsolved. This is due to the no-snitch culture respected by many in poor Black communities. Most Black people in these communities are reluctant to cooperate with police investigations because of negative cultural attitudes toward being a snitch, as well as fear of retaliation. In "the 'hood," they say, "snitches get stitches." So where are the BLM marches for justice for the thousands of Black lives taken due to homicide?

ABORTION—BLACK GENOCIDE

Another shocking Black body count we are not allowed to talk about is the staggering number of Black babies that are killed in the womb, murdered before they are even given a chance at life. An estimated one thousand Black babies are aborted every single day in America. This number accounts for a disproportionate number of total babies aborted. According to CDC data, Black women are only 6 percent of the population. Yet, abortions by Black women account for close to 40 percent of all abortions. In some states, up to 52 percent of Black babies are never born. That means Black women are having more abortions than they are giving birth.

Every year, approximately 380,000 Black people that would have otherwise entered the world are exterminated. This makes abortion the number one killer of Black lives, by far. To give you a visual, every year, abortion snuffs out the lives of approximately the same number of Black Americans as those that gathered to hear Dr. Martin Luther King Jr.'s speech, "I Have a Dream."

Dr. Alveda King, niece of Dr. Martin Luther King Jr., said, "The greatest irony is that abortion has done what the Klan only dreamed of."

Why are Black babies disproportionately aborted? The answer lies in the history of the origins of Planned Parenthood, the abortion clinic giant. Planned Parenthood was founded by democrat Margaret Sanger, who was known as a racist eugenicist. She wrote many articles about eugenics in the journal she founded in 1917. One of them was "The Birth Control Review," in which she advocated for women's health, saying, "Concerning Blacks, immigrants, and indigents, they are human weeds, reckless breeders... spawning human beings, who should have never been born."

On December 10, 1939, in a letter to Clarence Gable commenting on the "Negro Project," Sanger wrote, "We do not want word to go out that we want to exterminate the Negro population, and the minister is the man who can straighten out that idea if it ever occurs to any of their more rebellious members...."

In Margaret Sanger's own written words, Planned Parenthood was essentially founded to control the Black American population growth. Sadly, this mission is still underway. Today, the Democratic Party is still at the center of embracing this agenda. Not only does the Democratic Party fully embrace this racist organization, they also fervently promote it as a virtuous organization, as the centerpiece for women's reproductive health.

Hillary Clinton said, in an acceptance speech of Planned Parenthood's Margaret Sanger Award, "I admire Margaret Sanger enormously... I am really in awe of her."

In stark contrast, President Trump has been the most pro-life president in modern history. He is the first ever president to speak at a pro-life rally, where he unapologetically declared, "Every child is a scared gift from God. Every life is worth protecting."

If Black lives really matter, why isn't Planned Parenthood, Inc., an organization that has killed more than half the Black population, not of any concern to BLM or the Democratic Party?

These are the questions that need to be asked. It's clear that Black Lives Matter is only concerned with the Black lives that can be used to further their Marxist divide-and-conquer political agenda. Not all Black lives matter to them. Clearly the Black lives taken unjustly at the hands of other Black people don't matter to them, even though they represent the vast majority of casualties. Nor do the Black lives matter taken in the wombs.

In America, we don't have as big a race problem as we're led to believe; we have a disinformation problem. Much of the racial division we see has been manufactured and fomented by media hysteria. It's crucial that we Americans, of every race, resist falling into the trap of those who want to see our nation divided on racial lines. We must be objective and rational rather than acting out of emotion, every time the trap is set.

CHAPTER 8

DEFUND THE POLICE?
BAD IDEA OR BAIT AND SWITCH?

At the center of the demands made by The BLM movement is the call to abolish and defund the police. When I first heard this demand, I honestly thought it was satire. How did our country get to this?

If people think this is just a kooky slogan or hashtag being pushed by a fringe group of woke "journalists," activists, and academics on Twitter, they're dead wrong. It's apparent that this is a policy move that's being seriously pushed, embraced, and implemented by Democratic mayors and governors across the country.

According to a report by *The Hill*, in Minneapolis, Minnesota, where George Floyd died, the Minneapolis parks and recreation board, the city's school district, museums, the University of Minnesota, and other venues, all severed ties with the city police. This means no police protecting public schools, parks, and other venues throughout the city. Democratic Rep. Ilhan Omar said, "This does not go far enough!" She endorsed the idea of completely disbanding the Minneapolis Police Department, calling the department, "a cancer," and "rotten to the root"

During the official DNC convention, speakers even called for prisons to be abolished. These ideas, from defunding the police, to outright abolishing prisons, are being grafted into the Democratic Party platform, and we're seeing them begin to be implemented.

In July, Los Angeles Mayor Garcetti announced the city would be cutting the LAPD budget by 150 million dollars and using those funds for "reinvesting in Black communities and communities of color." No specifics on how that money would be used was offered.

The city of New York also cut the police budget, with devastating results to the city. After disbanding the NYPD anti-crime unit, the city saw shootings soar by 205 percent in July of 2020 over the same month the previous year.

Murders were also up by 79 percent, and burglaries were up by 34 percent. The explosion of crime in New York is only partially due to the defunding of the police. The increase in crime is also symptomatic of other progressive policies that have been slowly implemented by the city's far-left mayors. These include bail reform, which allows criminals to be released without bail; the emptying out of prisons due to Covid; and the lackadaisical approach to prosecuting criminals.

Ironically, defunding the police disparately harms poor Black communities the most. It leaves Black lives defenseless against criminals and more vulnerable to gang violence.

The idea peddled by the progressive left that Black neighborhoods are being over policed is wrong. Based on the statistics, Blacks are arrested at about the same rate that victims of crimes identify blacks as the perpetrators of the crime. The victims have no reason to lie about who the perpetrator was. So, if Black neighborhoods were being over policed, then there would be a large discrepancy in those two numbers.

One tragic victim of the increase in crime in New York that caught my attention was that of thirteen-month-old baby, Davell Gardner, who was shot in his stroller while at a cookout in

Brooklyn. Two men reportedly stepped out of an SUV and opened fire at the cookout. Little Davell was gravely wounded after a bullet struck him in his stomach. He was rushed to the hospital where he died a few hours later.

Davell's grandmother said, "They need to stop this gun violence." She went on to say, "I feel like this: You all are ranting and raving about Black lives. But you take a life that was only a year and half old…and it's not fair!"

A Gallup poll conducted from June 23 to July 6 of 2020 surveyed more than thirty-six thousand US adults. The pollsters report that 81 percent of Black Americans said "they would like to see police presence stay the same or increase in their communities." This shows the gap and disconnect between the loud voices of far-left activists in movements like BLM and ordinary Black people who live in these communities riddled with violence, particularly those with children that have to navigate the dangers of having to go to work, pass the drug house on the way to school, and deal with neighborhood crime.

Some Black Americans are forced to sleep on the floor at night for fear that bullets might be shot through the wall. The bullets are not fired by White supremacists. The bullets are fired by other Black men. But it isn't the victim's voices that are amplified. The voices that are blasted on repeat are that of the BLM activists calling for reduction or eradication of police. They are amplified by the media and presented as representative of the Black community at large.

I believe this disconnect can also be viewed through a racial lens, if you consider that the plurality of those in the BLM movement are affluent White liberals, mostly women. Pew research found that only one in six protestors in the demonstrations and rioting were Black.

The findings align with comments made by BET founder, Robert Johnson, who noted that most Black Americans "laugh at White people attempting to bring down monuments and cancel everything they deem to be 'racist.'"

Johnson also said that White people "have the mistaken assumption that Black people are sitting around cheering for them saying 'Oh, my God, look at these White people. They're doing something so important to us. They're taking down the statue of a Civil War general who fought for the South."

When a person calls 911, the police don't ask the race of the person needing their help. They're trained to immediately head toward whatever situation they've been called to, no matter how dangerous it is. Police put their lives at risk to save people of every race and color, every day.

A close friend of mine is married to a police officer. She recently broke down in tears. She was grief stricken at how police officers went from being viewed as heroes to being portrayed as the worst elements of America. She was heartbroken. She knows that is not who her husband is. As the wife of a policeman, she lives with the possibility that there could come a day when her husband may not come home because he has put himself in harm's way, in service to the predominantly Black community he serves.

Are there bad cops and corrupt police? Yes, there are. Like any other profession, there are good and bad people. There are good teachers and bad teachers. But the teaching profession is never defined by the bad teachers. So why are all police officers being painted with a broad brush and defined by the bad actors in their profession?

Police brutality is real. But there's no evidence to suggest that it's as widespread as portrayed by the media, or that the brutality is racially motivated.

One thing that is not reported in the media is the diversity of many of the police departments that are being labeled as "systemically racist."

The NYPD, which is the largest police department in the country, is 54 percent White, 23 percent Black, 24 percent Hispanic, and 4 percent Asian. In fact, Black Americans are overrepresented in the police department, as they make up only 16 percent of the NYC population. In LA, 46 percent of the police are Latino, and only 32 percent are White. The rest are Black and Asian.

The chief of the Minneapolis Police Department, where George Floyd was killed, is a Black man. So, the notion that police departments are racist, White supremacist institutions that are out to hunt down and kill Black people for the crime of being Black is simply not true.

We can have a discussion on better policing and the measures that should be implemented to ensure bad cops can be easily reported, fired, and even prosecuted. However, the manipulation of the facts, and the subsequent demonization of all police by the left and their allies in the media is dangerous and harmful to the peace and security of America.

In 2019, America's eight hundred thousand police officers had over 375 million encounters with citizens. The overwhelming majority of these encounters were positive or uneventful. Yet, the media cherry picks the handful of incidents involving police brutality and highlights them to make it appear to represent common police behavior. This manipulation of perception creates a narrative that has been destructive to race relations in America.

The consequences of this false narrative, perpetrated by the media, can be dangerous. Police officers become targets, and surges in shootings of officers follows. Because of the lawless attitude toward authority being fomented, some Black Americans now feel justified in resisting police. The consequence is more violent clashes between blacks and the police.

When police officers come under attack, the way they have been, it adversely affects policing. Their willingness to do proactive policing, exiting their squad cars, and interacting with civilians, drops dramatically. This is known as the *Ferguson effect,* which refers to an increase in violent crime rates in a community caused by reduced pro-active policing due to the community's distrust and hostility towards the police. The term was coined by Doyle Sam Dotson III, the chief of the St. Louis, MO police department, to explain an increased murder rate in some U.S. cities following the Ferguson riots. The stats show that less policing leads to more violent crime and homicides, in the mostly Black communities they serve. In conclusion, defunding/abolishing the police is a policy that hurts poor Black people more than any other demographic.

POLICE BRUTALITY AND THE FACTS

In the wake of George Floyd's death, allegedly caused by the actions of a Minnesota police officer, we have been bombarded with reports of widespread police brutality. We're told that police officers systematically target Black Americans for death. The lie that White police officers are engaged in genocide against Black men is promoted by many in the media, academia, and sports and entertainment.

So, what are the real numbers? How many unarmed Black men were killed by police last year? If we're using a word like genocide, it must be nine hundred thousand-plus. In 2019, police shot and killed a total of nine unarmed Black men. Nine. This doesn't mean they shot nine innocent men who were just minding their business. In fact, in most of the cases, the police were called to a crime scene that resulted in the perpetrator resisting arrest and engaging in an altercation with the police that ultimately resulted in their being shot and killed.

In the same year, police also shot and killed nineteen White unarmed men. This is according to data published by the *Washington Post*. The *Post* goes on to note that these 2019 numbers are down from the thirty-eight unarmed Blacks and thirty-two unarmed Whites shot in 2015.

The pushback to these numbers is that Black men are being disproportionately killed by the police. BLM argues that blacks account for only 13 percent of the overall population, while Whites make up 63 percent. The problem with this rebuttal is that it doesn't take into account the fact that Black people are also disproportionately committing more violent crime.

According to the 2018 FBI crime data, Black Americans made up 53 percent of homicide offenders and committed about 60 percent of the robberies, despite being only 13 percent of the population. In 2019, there were approximately fifteen thousand homicides in America. More than half of those homicides were Black victims killed by other Black people, as we discussed in earlier chapters.

As a result of high crime rates in Black neighborhoods, Black people are likely to have more police encounters per capita than Whites or other races. Black people call 911 more than any other race. So, police are responding to calls from where the crimes are occurring.

When you look at the numbers and take all the data into account, you find that police are not disproportionately killing Black men. The data and the evidence do not support the false narrative that Black people should fear for their lives when they have an encounter with a police officer. The claim that it is systemic racism that makes it more likely that a person will be shot by the police is absurd. The truth is that an individual's criminal behavior, not his race, is the determining factor.

It's also important to note that, according to FBI data published by the *Wall Street Journal*, police officers are eighteen times more likely to be killed by a Black man than an unarmed Black male is to be killed by a police officer. So, the misconception that police shooting Black men is a regular occurrence and a typical experience for Black Americans is a myth that has been propagated by the progressive left in the media, academia, and entertainment.

They selectively spotlight only incidents of unarmed Black men being killed by police, while ignoring incidents of Whites killed by the police. The result is that a distorted picture of reality is presented to the people.

If the media provided a fair and balanced coverage of all police shootings, then the perception that race is the main driver of police shootings would be shattered. But the media is not interested in providing any such context, because they have an ideological agenda and narrative to push.

When unarmed White men are shot by police, it rarely makes the national news. Take the case of Dillon Taylor, a twenty-one-year-old unarmed White man who was shot and killed by a police officer.

The officer who shot Dillon, Bron Cruz, was cleared of all wrongdoing, as the shooting was deemed justified. On the afternoon of the fatal shooting, Officer Cruz responded to reports of an armed man in the area. Cruz approached Taylor, who had his hands in his waist band under his shirt. Because he fit the description, Taylor was asked to put his hands in the air to which he responded, "No, fool," and continued to walk.

When Taylor turned around and removed his hands from this waistband, Cruz shot him twice. The prosecutor concluded that even though Taylor was unarmed, the mere fact that officer Cruz thought he had a weapon and that he would use it against him, was enough to clear the officer of any wrongdoing.

In another case, police in Buffalo, New York, threw Martin Gugino, an unarmed, seventy-five-year-old White man to the ground. He cracked his head on the sidewalk and the cops left him lying there, bleeding from the ears.

These are just two of a multitude of examples involving unarmed White men being brutalized or dying at the hands of police, that never gains any national attention. If Taylor and Gugino were Black, their stories would have received wall to wall coverage for weeks in the national news.

This selective and distorted media coverage has worked well for a political party that benefits from keeping Black people in a perpetual state of fear, believing that racism is the biggest issue they face. Every election cycle, the Democratic Party pose as the ones who will save Black people from the racist boogeymen. Once elected, they proceed to do absolutely nothing that solves any issues of substance in the Black community.

Not only does the left benefit from this narrative politically but racism is an entire lucrative industry that brings in billions of dollars per year. The race baiting hustle has made numerous political operatives, authors, pundits, journalists, and activists very wealthy.

Black conservative commentator and author Candace Owens spoke on this during a speech in which she called out political "race hustlers" in media, entertainment, and politics who have "extorted Black pain to line [their] own pockets and blindfolded the Black youth against seeing the opportunities that lay beneath their feet here in America the land of the free and home of the brave."

Black intellectual and author Thomas Stowell famously said it best: "Racism is not dead, but it is on life support—kept alive by politicians, race hustlers and people who get a sense of superiority by denouncing others as 'racist.'"

CHAPTER 9

THE CHURCH—WHERE *WE* HAVE FAILED

For decades, the church in America has taken itself out of the political and cultural conversations to the detriment of the nation. The void left by the church has allowed the progressive left to advance and systematically push through their agenda. Over the last fifty-plus years, this has occurred with very little to no resistance from the church or from political conservatives.

In 1954, a provision in the US tax code introduced by then Democratic Senator Lyndon B. Johnson (LBJ) was the catalyst. The provision prohibited all non-profits (read, Christian churches and organizations) from speaking in favor of any political candidate. This key but forgotten event paved the way for the increased squelching of free speech and the gradual withdrawal of the church from the political sphere.

The church not having a political voice is something that has bothered me a great deal. I believe it is our duty as Christians to have a voice that brings about the light of God's kingdom to the world around us in all spheres, including cultural and political ones.

An example of the church having a political voice would be speaking on issues like the bloodshed of the unborn. In 2018, New York state officials signed into law a bill that permits abortion all the way up to the day of birth. There was a deafening silence from the church for the most part. Where was the national outcry? Even something this egregious did not motivate the church-at-large to speak on behalf of those who are not able to speak for themselves.

Abortion is a horrific atrocity taking place in America. 62 million people have aborted since the Roe v. Wade court decision in 1973. The blood shed not only has natural consequences, it also has very serious spiritual consequences over the nation.

THE GREAT COMMISSION

> "Then Jesus came to them and said, All authority in Heaven and on Me. Therefore go and make disciples of all nations, baptizing them in the name of the Father, and of the Son, and of the Holy Spirit, and teaching them to obey all that I have commanded you. And surely, I am with you always, even to the end of the age" (Matt. 28:18–20).

This is the great commission. Notice in this verse that Jesus commands His church to not only make disciples of individuals but to also make disciples of entire nations, teaching the nations to obey all that He taught us. This means, the American church is called to disciple and influence America as a nation to establish God's kingdom, and His will for this nation. Unfortunately, the church has, for the most part, failed at this. Instead, the church has focused on discipling and making converts of just individuals, while neglecting the mandate to disciple the nation as a whole.

There are several reasons why the church has failed to influence the nation in the last sixty years. One of the reasons is that the eschatology in the modern American church has been that of escapism. This is the eschatological doctrine that says that things are meant to just get worse and worse as we approach the end times, and there's nothing we can do about it, except wait for Jesus to rapture us out of this world at any moment.

Even though the doctrine of the rapture is biblical, this escapism mentality in the church has resulted in an apathetic church. In general, the church has not felt the need to engage in the world for the Kingdom of God or fulfill its mandate to disciple and influence the direction of the nation. If you live your life as a Christian with the doctrine that you are going to leave any minute in the rapture, then you are less likely to make an investment to change the world around you for the better.

This way of thinking neglects what Jesus called us Christians to do in Luke 19:13, which is to "occupy till I come." Jesus also said we are to be the salt of the Earth.

Again, Jesus says, "You are the salt of the earth. But if the salt loses its saltiness, how can it be made salty again? It is no longer good for anything, except to be thrown out and trampled by men" (Matt. 5:13, NIV).

In the first century, in the Middle East, salt served two purposes. In addition to making food more flavorful, because refrigeration had not been invented, salt was also used to preserve food. Believers in Christ are preservatives to the world, preserving it from Satan's perverted kingdom.

THE SEVEN MIND MOLDERS OF CULTURE

What does occupying, being the salt and the light, and discipling a nation, look like in practical terms for the church? In his book *Invading Babylon*, Dr. Lance Wallnau, a Christian author, states, "Discipling a nation, involves the church influencing the seven spheres or seven mind molders of culture."

He makes the case that these, "Seven spheres are what molds the minds of the people and therefore shapes the culture and direction of a nation. These seven spheres of influence are:

1. Family
2. Education
3. Government
4. Media (TV, newspapers, internet, radio)
5. Arts, Entertainment, Sports
6. Business
7. Religion."

To disciple a nation, the church needs to have significant influence in these seven spheres or mind molders of cultures. Today, the church and conservatives alike, have very little to no influence in at least six of these spheres. We are barely holding on to the seventh, which is religion, as churches become more secular and liberal.

Up until the 1950s, the church was very influential in shaping American culture. This was evident in family structures, in the education system, and could even be seen in entertainment. All seven spheres of influence were largely influenced by conservative Christian values.

The first 230 universities and colleges in America were established for the education and development of Christians and ministers. Most of the Ivy League universities and colleges, like Harvard and Yale, were founded by Christians for Christians. Now these institutions are radically far left and even hostile to Christianity and conservatism. What happened?

At some point in the 1960s, the church in America decided that it was not going to engage in the culture anymore. As the liberal movements grew in the 1960s, and gained influence in most of these spheres, they were met with little to no resistance from the church.

In 1962, the left succeeded in removing prayer and Bible reading from school with a Supreme Court case that was decided not by the majority of Americans, but by a vote of eight Supreme Court Justices. Since then, there has been a gradual and relentless effort to completely remove God from the public square. A most recent example is the removal of the words, "So help me God!" from the House of Representatives witness' swearing-in before testifying.

So, from education, government, media and entertainment, the church has slowly but surely lost its influence in our culture. In effect, the church abdicated its mandate to occupy the territory it had inherited from the Christian founding of the nation. Instead, without a fight, the church surrendered the ground to the enemy. Instead of maintaining its influence, the church took the approach of focusing on building their own kingdoms and ministries.

From this, we have seen the rise of churches that look inward and focus solely on bringing people into the church to be converted. As a result of this approach, the church lost its cultural power, because it focused on changing the world from within the church rather than releasing the church into these world spheres of influence. Jesus plainly teaches us to "go out into the world." Dr. Lance Wallnau puts it perfectly: "The goal isn't to pull a convert out of the world and into the church, as we so often do. The Goal is to be the church that raises up disciples who go into all the world."

As the church has gotten this wrong and disengaged, it has left a void that has been quickly filled by other influences. The result of this decades long neglect of cultural relevance by the church have been devastating. The chickens are now coming home to roost. We now find ourselves in a world where basic biblical principles that were universally agreed on as little as five to ten years ago—principles like the idea that there are only two genders, are now controversial.

The removal of prayer and Bible study from school is another example. Following the 1963 removal of prayer and the Bible from schools, we have seen devastating results. According to data compiled by CNSNews, drawing on research by the CDC and the Family Research Council, here are some of the effects that occurred among young people, families, and education following the 1963 decision:

A. Young people
   - Teen pregnancies increased 187 percent
   - For girls ages ten to fourteen, pregnancies are up 553 percent since 1963
   - Sexually transmitted diseases among teens are up 226 percent since 1936
B. Family
   - After 1963, divorces increased by 300 percent each year for fifteen years
   - Single parent families went up 140 percent in the years following 1963
   - Unmarried people living together increased 353 percent in the years following 1963
C. The nation:
   - Violent crime has increased 544 percent since 1963
   - Illegal drug use has become an enormous problem
D. Education:
   - Academic achievement and SAT scores have dropped exponentially since 1963
   - Deterioration of school behavior; Comparison between the top four complaints of teachers from 1940 to

1962, talking, chewing gum, making noise, running in the halls

Education expert William Jeynes, a professor at California State College in Long Beach and a senior fellow at the Witherspoon Institute in Princeton, New Jersey, spoke at the Heritage Foundation, in Washington, DC, on Aug. 13, 2014 about putting the Bible and prayer back into US public schools.

He said, "One can argue, and some have, that the decision by the Supreme Court—in a series of three decisions back in 1962 and 1963—to remove Bible and prayer from our public schools, may be the most spiritually significant event in our nation's history over the course of the last fifty five years."

George Washington, one of our Founding Fathers, said this about removing religious principles from society: "Let us, with caution, indulge the supposition that morality can be maintained without religion. Reason and experience, both forbid us to expect that national morality can prevail, in exclusion of religious principle...."

This played out during the racial crisis this year. Because the church has lost so much influence and relevance in today's culture, it was completely caught off guard. The response to the racial events that took place this year has been from a place of complete political ignorance.

For decades, the church has operated in its own little bubble, willfully oblivious and disengaged from the world around it. As life rages on, cultural conversations are happening about the definitions of marriage, abortion, gender, race, etc. During this critical time, many church pastors have quietly avoided these relevant topics. They do so in order that they not offend half their congregations.

The moment you take a stance, on any issue one way or another, you're bound to offend at least some of the people in your church. In recent years, the culture of many churches has been "seeker friendly." This means the church wants to appeal to new, unchurched seekers, with a more sugar-coated kingdom message that's not offensive. But God's truth is offensive to the world. Jesus offended some of the people everywhere He went with the truth of the Gospel.

As I mentioned earlier, the Johnson Amendment of 1954 played a major role in shifting the church's engagement in political issues. Prior to the Johnson Amendment, churches had a long-standing tradition of being outspoken and involved in the political activity of the day. It was even commonplace for pastors to preach about political issues and even endorse candidates.

Like every other battle the church has lost, this assault on the freedom of speech of the church and its leaders was met with little resistance. For over sixty years, the church has been silenced on issues that affect us politically. This was true at least up until May of 2017, when President Trump signed an executive order ostensibly relaxing enforcement of the Johnson Amendment, saying, "I will get rid of and totally destroy the Johnson Amendment and allow our representatives of faith to speak freely and without fear of retribution."

If the church fails to address relevant issues and national conversations that are taking place and are affecting people in their everyday lives, then the church becomes tone deaf and irrelevant.

We are called to be "the salt and light of the Earth." This means we are to dispel darkness by shining our light on issues facing the world.

If the church is silent, then other voices fill the void. These voices gladly shepherd America away from God's will. This is what I saw taking place during the racial protests and riots. The church's initial response to the racial upheaval the nation was experiencing was very disappointing. It's very awkward, because for so long the church has kept itself out of any cultural or political debates. Now, all the sudden, in response to an abundance of pressure, they were faced with having to say something. I saw churches that had never taken a stance on any political issue, make a knee-jerk reaction, jumping on the Black Lives Matter bandwagon.

The tragic death of George Floyd, and the events that followed, shocked the whole nation. Many churches, in their genuine attempt to empathize with the situation, embraced and followed the world's lead instead of leading themselves.

As the body of Christ, we must resist the temptation to do what's popular with the world in an effort to be embraced by secular culture. "And be not conformed to this world: but be ye transformed by the renewing of your mind" (Rom. 12:2). We are not called to conform to this world and its remedies for societal issues; we are called to be set apart. Jesus said, if we truly follow him, we will be hated by the world for his name sake not embraced.

CRITICAL RACE THEORY AND THE CHURCH

The result of coming into agreement with the world's remedies for what is taking place in the area of race relations is that the church has been infiltrated by critical race theory. This destructive ideology is now being introduced into the church under the guise of "racial reconciliation." Unfortunately, it's starting to gain a foothold within many churches.

As described in chapter six, critical race theory teaches that American culture is rife with White supremacy and baked-in racism, and it's used to hold people of color back. African American pastor and talk-show host Abraham Hamilton acknowledges that CRT is the philosophy behind identity politics and comes straight out of the Marxist playbook. He explained recently, on American Family Radio: "[CRT] doesn't depend on your personal feeling, sentiment, [or] heart condition—it's based on the group that you're born into.... It completely eliminates individual responsibility, individual sin and expands it to corporate sin. And based on how you're born, you are immediately ascribed into an 'oppressor' or 'oppressed' group."

He goes on to say that critical race theory is being widely introduced into the church as something that it is not. "The traditional definition and applications are not being used initially, as a way to first get a toe in the door." Hamilton contends that "it's a bait-and-switch tactic that is corrupting the faith and an assault on the key tenet of evangelicalism."

CRT is a dangerous Marxist worldview that is antithetical to Christianity. It emphasizes the ways that people differ from each other, while ignoring, if not rejecting altogether, what the Bible says about the commonality of humans. Among these commonalities is the fact that the Bible teaches that, "we all (every race, nation, tongue and tribe) are sinners."

> "For there is no distinction: for all have sinned and
> fall short of the glory of God" (Rom. 3:22–23).

But these words from the Bible did not stop the Southern Baptist Convention (SBC)—the largest protestant denomination in America—from officially adopting critical race theory and intersectionality as analytical tools to be used in "fostering racial reconciliation in the church."

CHURCH OF BLM

This embrace of CRT, social justice, and BLM have become a new religion unto itself. Sadly, many Christians and churches who want to be embraced by the world are converting en masse.

It is crucial that Christians have the discernment to view this movement for what it is really is. It's not just a social movement for justice. We must recognize it for what it is at its core—a spiritual movement and a religion.

BLM lists their demands in a manifesto that uses intrinsically eschatological language to describe a vision of the world they want to see manifest. They call for a fundamentally different world. BLM is not merely some harmless, innocuous hashtag that looks good on social media. According to the founders of BLM, it's a spiritual world view.

Apart from declaring that they are trained Marxists, it has come to light that the founders of the BLM movement practice witchcraft, black magic, and regularly summon dead spirits. One of the three founding members of BLM, Patrisse Cullors, said, "I'm calling for spirituality to be deeply radical.... We're not just having a social justice movement; this is a spiritual movement."

In a Zoom-type meeting between Cullors and Dr. Melina Abdullah, a professor of African studies at California State University in Los Angeles and founder of BLM's LA chapter, Abudllah said, "We've become very intimate with the spirits that we call on regularly. Each of them seems to have a different presence and personality. You know, I laugh a lot with Wakiesha.... I didn't meet her in her body, right? I met her through this work."

Black conservative Christian podcast host Abraham Hamilton said, "the Black Lives Matter movement engages in 'witchcraft.'" He called on "Christians who have allied themselves with the organization to rethink their decision."

After playing an audio piece of the Zoom conversation of the BLM leaders, Hamilton concluded that the conversation proves that Black Lives Matter leaders are "summoning the spirits of the dead, using the power of the spirits of the dead, in order to give them the ability to do what they're calling the so-called justice work."

Hamilton contends that the leaders seeking to summon the spirits of the dead are adhering to the Yoruba religion of Ifa, an ancient West African religion. In the audio piece, BLM co-founder Abdullah is heard discussing the spiritual purpose of their say-her-name chant. "When people chant the names of those slain by police, they invoke that spirit...and those spirits actually become present with you."

Following these statements, Abdullah led a group of demonstrators in a ritual at a recent protest outside of Los Angeles Mayor Eric Garcetti's home. As part of the ritual, people recited the names of those they claimed were "taken by state violence before their time and ancestors [were] now being called back to animate their own justice."

In condemning BLM's spiritual practices, Hamilton cited Deuteronomy 18. The Old Testament chapter describes those who practice witchcraft or call upon the dead as "detestable to the Lord."

SALVATION VIA BLM

BLM is also soteriological in nature. Soteriology is the study of salvation—how one is saved. If you're saved and you're righteous, then you're justified, and the just inherit eternal life. And in this instance, Black Lives Matter offers the world-at-large a societal salvation and deliverance from the current world into the "fundamentally different world" they envision. As the righteous arbiters of this salvation, BLM is in effect saying, based on black people's ethnicity and race, they're sinless and guiltless, and there is an aspect of holiness to their skin color because of the past they've endured here in America.

Darrell Harrison, a Black host of *Just Thinking*, a Christian podcast, said, "The words "Black Lives Matter" are not just three innocuous words, but that these words represent a world view." He goes on to say, "It's a Trojan horse, that far too many pastors are repeating, not recognizing that what they're advocating is fundamentally a worldview, which the dictionary defines as, a comprehensive conception of the world in which we live from a specific standpoint. As believers, we are taught a biblical worldview."

Our worldview, as believers, is antithetical to the Marxist orthodoxy of critical race theory. The biblical worldview stands in contradiction to the concepts of collective and permanent White guilt. This condition is permanent because there is no possibility of redemption according to CRT. The Gospel of BLM is a works-based salvation that never truly saves the sinner from the sin of being born White.

Ultimately, on any given issue, as Christians, we have to reconcile and evaluate all things through the lens of what God's Word has to say. BLM is not a movement that any Christian should align with. BLM is indeed a spiritual movement that is not of God. It is a movement that is based on the doctrines of the neo-Marxist critical race theory, which is at odds with every precept and principle of our Christian faith.

HOW THE CHURCH SHOULD RESPOND

In his classic work *Institutes of the Christian Religion*, John Calvin said, "We should judge nothing to be exceptional or worthy of praise, unless we recognize that it comes from God."

In all things as believers, we are to discern spiritual things and recognize if something is of God or not. "Beloved, do not believe every spirit, but test the spirits to see whether they are from God, for many false prophets have gone out into the world" (1 John 4:1).

We must have discernment because many things appear to be good on the surface. 2 Corinthians 11:14 states that "even Satan disguises himself as an angel of light." This means that not all light is from God. When held up against the test of Scripture, Black Lives Matter and CRT clearly fails that test.

God commands believers to "speak…truth in love" (Eph. 4:15). Now more than ever, in a generation where the truth is not popular with the world, the church must have the courage to speak the truth in love. We have all lived in the era of Western civilization. For centuries, biblical foundations and principles have been the norm. In recent years, we have seen the rise of movements that are making great strides in their war against these biblical foundations.

America needs a revival and a reformation. The revival will be an outpouring of the Spirit. But the reformation will only happen if the church forms an organized, strategic resistance to evil. The church must take back territory and reoccupy the spheres of influence that have been lost to the enemy over the last six decades.

When I first heard about the teaching on the seven spheres of influence, it really resonated with me. I thought it was brilliant. I can't believe how wrong we have been for so long. I started to see, in my own life, how God was calling me out of the business sphere and into the political sphere.

Everything that happened in the last seven years has been by the hand of God, shepherding me toward my calling in politics. Every door in my business was shut, which caused a lot of uncertainty and fear. But at the same time, God has been opening doors for me in politics. So, the message of the seven spheres of influence has helped me to understand my place in God's purpose for my life. It is God's plan to bring His Kingdom on Earth. It is my job to be obedient to His call.

I can imagine how much better the world would be if each Christian were using their God given gifts to live out their destiny and purpose within the sphere God calls them to. The quest of every Christian should be to find out why God has put them on Earth at this time in history and to live out that destiny.

The way the church has treated giftings is that gifts are to be used within the local church. For example, if you are a gifted filmmaker or actor, then your calling is to be in the church's Christmas play. This is not a bad thing, however, if you are living out the great commission to disciple nations, you are to take your gift to the world and use it to influence culture in the sphere of entertainment. For example, if your gift is acting or filmmaking, you should be in the film industry, whether in Hollywood or elsewhere, influencing the film industry and the movies being produced.

Likewise, those called to teaching must go into the education sphere as a mission field that needs to be occupied to bring the light of God's Kingdom. That which God has gifted you with is not just so you have a job; it's also your calling and purpose to bring light, hope, and the goodness of God to the world.

We're called to advance the Kingdom of God and bring light to a dark world. Jesus taught us to pray, "Thy kingdom come. Thy will be done on Earth as it is in heaven" (Matt. 6:10). In his book, *Invading Babylon*, Dr. Lance Walnau reminds us that "the purpose God gave Adam was to be fruitful, multiply and have dominion over the earth. After Adam partook of the forbidden fruit, Satan was able to usurp Adam's authority over the Earth and take dominion himself. He had his way over humanity until Jesus came. Jesus came to reconcile us back to God and replace Satan's perverse kingdom with the Kingdom of God."

So, because of what Christ did, it's now the responsibility of God's people, empowered by the Holy Spirit, to regain the dominion that Adam lost and displace the dark deeds of Satan in family, education, politics, entertainment, etc.

The approach of just building churches and praying people will come to church on Sunday and be transformed is insufficient. Every member of the body of Christ is a full-time minister of the Gospel. Your ministry is lived out daily, in whatever sphere of influence you are called to.

Movements like BLM are gaining prominence because they are actively engaged in culture and they give people a false sense of being a part of something bigger than themselves. If the church is not relevant, then movements like BLM have a monopoly on culture.

As the church, it is important that we play our part in the national conversation. We must offer biblical solutions to the cultural answers people are seeking. We must speak the truth in love, while serving and engaging the world around us.

The problem is that our theology has been so flawed. Author and American reformed pastor David Chilton made this accurate assessment of where the church has been theologically:

A very common evangelical worldview is that "the Earth is the devil's, and the fullness thereof"—that the world belongs to Satan, and that Christians can expect only defeat until the Lord returns. And that is exactly the lie that Satan wants Christians to believe. If God's people think the devil is winning, it makes his job just that much easier. What would he do if Christians stopped retreating and started advancing against him?

James 4:7 tells us what he would do: he would "flee" from us! So why isn't the devil fleeing from us in this age?"

"Why are Christians at the mercy of Satan and his servants? Why aren't Christians conquering kingdoms with the Gospel, as they did in times past? Because Christians are not resisting the devil! Worse yet, they're being told by their pastors and leaders not to resist, but to retreat instead! Christian leaders have turned James 4:7 inside out, and are really giving aid and comfort to the enemy because they are, in effect, saying to the devil: "Resist the church, and we will flee from you!"

And Satan is taking them at their word. So then, when Christians see themselves losing on every front, they take it as "proof" that God has not promised to give dominion to His people. But the only thing it proves is that James 4:7 is true after all, including its flip side—that is, if you don't resist the devil, he won't flee from you."

Christians are a majority in this country, yet we have little relevance and influence on culture. To effect change in society, a people group need not even be a majority. The LGBTQ+ movement is a perfect example of a tiny minority group that has been able to invade and shift culture in their favor.

Whether you approve of them or not, they are extremely effective.

In the past ten years, the LGBTQ+ activists have become the most influential in every sphere of society. Just think about their influence on media, entertainment, art, family, politics, and business. Now they're making inroads into our education system. California is the first state to introduce gay history into the public school curriculum. Transgenderism is now being introduced to preschoolers and promoted to students in public schools across the country. Drag queens, aka men wearing dresses, now have their own designated "drag queen story time," where they get to read to your preschoolers at over twenty-two thousand public libraries in America. (I challenge you to do a search on this issue. You will be shocked.)

This advance on culture by the LBGTQ did not happen by chance. Represented by only 2 percent of the nation's population, the LGBTQ movement, in a relatively short period of time, has strategically gained massive influence in all spheres of society. The Church should have this level of strategy and commitment to influencing culture for the Kingdom of God.

Evangelist and author Dr. Lance Wallnau says there are three keys to changing culture:

"1.) The number one key to transforming a culture is to change the way people think.

2.) The number one way you change the way people think? You have to engage in what William Wilberforce called 'a sustained pattern of public persuasion.'

3.) This public persuasion needs to specifically penetrate the gates of influence where media, laws, celebrities and funding can push your ideas.

This is how America has been discipled in the last decade. We are not strong in these gates, but God can do things we can't and if we do our part and advance each in our own courageous way, the enemy will flee from us."

Education is an example of an important sphere that the Body of Christ must regain influence in to make a significant difference in culture and in people's lives. When the church had influence on education, teen suicides, teen pregnancy and even divorce rates were at their lowest.

We, the Body of Christ influencing religion, family, education, media, art and entertainment, business and politics is a revolutionary revelation that will transform the nation to fulfil its God given destiny as the beacon of light, hope and freedom. The Bible says the nations are Christ's in hesitance (Psalms. 2:8). America can be one of those nations that radiates the light of God's Kingdom once again. Only when and if each of us in the body of Christ becomes a light in the sphere in which God has called us to be that light.

CHAPTER 10

THE TOP SOLUTION— SCHOOL CHOICE

I n 2020, at the height of the Covid-19 lockdowns, I attended a re-open America rally. It was there that I met a fiery, black Trump supporter who has since become a good friend and a mentor, of sorts. She has an amazing story of redemption. Lisa was once a flaming progressive, pro-abortion, atheist, and radical feminist. She was also a top messaging strategist for the NAACP and ACLU. One day, she had a supernatural encounter with God that started a two-year journey of total transformation and deprograming of everything she once stood for.

As one of the most strategic political thinkers I've ever met, she has made such an impression on me. Having previously been on the left, she was extensively trained on political strategy. She often expresses frustration at the absence of strategy and planning she witnesses on the right. This is so true. The lack of organization and strategy on the right is the main reason why we win some battles here and there but continue to lose the war. Yes, we are losing the war.

One day, Lisa asked me, "What have conservatives/Christians won politically in the last hundred years?"

I began to name off some of the political victories, including the election of President Trump. She rightfully said, "Those are battles we have won, but the war against the erosion of the foundational values and principles that makes this country exceptional, is being lost. The war is being lost. Just take a look at the momentum and direction the country has been going for last hundred years. It's been ideologically in one direction only—to the left."

This statement was soberingly true. She further illustrated her point by using the famous "Chocolate Factory" episode of the classic sitcom *I Love Lucy*.

In the episode, Lucy yearns to make a name for herself and earn a living outside of housework. Ricky, her husband, agrees to change places with her for a week. Ethel, Lucy's best friend, joins her at the local candy factory, where they wreak havoc. Their task is simple: pick up and wrap the chocolate candies as they move along an ever-faster conveyor belt. As the conveyor belt speeds up, the comedy ensues. It starts off slowly, then goes faster and faster. The ladies can't keep up. In an effort to conceal their ineffectiveness, they hilariously stuff the chocolates into their mouths, under their hats, and even into their bras, lest a tough forewoman fire them for incompetence.

Lisa asked me, "How many characters are in that scene?" The obvious answer is that there are three: the forewoman, Lucy, and Ethel. Wrong! "The correct answer is four. The fourth character is the conveyor belt," Lisa said. You see, Lucy and Ethel represent the Republicans, Christians, and conservatives. Each piece of chocolate, represents the issues we're fighting for, whether it's ending abortion, gun rights, immigration, lower taxes, deregulation, religious liberty, etc.

The ubiquitous conveyor belt represents the left's agenda, which continues to move forward and to the left. In the meantime, conservatives, represented by Lucy and Ethel, are at the end of the conveyor belt, trying to pick up each person coming off the belt and convince them of conservative policy/cultural issue one at a time. Conservative Christians are able to pick off the belt a few here and there. However, they're unable to keep up with the speed of the belt and the numbers because the momentum and the trajectory represented by the conveyor belt belongs to, and is controlled by, the progressive left.

The left control this momentum and the ideological direction of the country because the conveyor belt ultimately represents the left's control over the education system.

Ouch! This was a wakeup call for me. Every year, the public school system pumps out left-wing foot soldiers. These students have spent six hours or more per day, for thirteen years, in public schools. More so now than before, they are systematically indoctrinated to be on the left of every issue that we as conservatives want to conserve in our culture.

Christians and conservatives teach their children one set of values at home, then they send them off to a public school. There they are taught a conflicting set of values that are at odds with the values instilled in them at home and at church.

Sadly, most parents don't even know what their children are being taught in school. They blindly trust that their children are safe in the hands of public-school educators. Academics and sports are what many parents focus on when considering a school. But they neglect the fact that the values being instilled in their children at school is equally consequential, if not more.

American children routinely attend thirteen years of public school and then four years of college, also run by far-left progressives and secular humanists. Then, over Thanksgiving dinner, Christian and conservative parents are routinely shocked to learn their that children have abandoned not only their faith in God but the conservative values they were raised with.

For Christians, God is the fundamental source of all truth, whether religious, academic, or otherwise. Public school teachers are not legally allowed to teach God's relationship to these fields of knowledge. This implies that God is not the source of all knowledge and truth. By the end of high school, God has been left out of every meaningful field of knowledge. So, it is of no surprise that many young people decide that God never really fits in the first place.

Even before I became politically savvy, it was a critical decision to place my children in a private Christian school, where teachers and administrators partner with parents for the sake of growing and maturing your children. A place that points out God's miraculous creation is at the center of everything.

The financial sacrifice to educate our children at a private Christian school was made in part because my mother made the same sacrifice for me. It is a big financial sacrifice indeed. But realistically, the investment in our children's future ability to critically think and defend their belief system, is worth every penny.

THE LEFT'S CONVEYOR-BELT MOMENTUM

The analogy of the conveyor belt is powerful, because it illustrates this fact: as long as the conveyor belt keeps moving in the left's predetermined direction, we're losing the war to conserve the constitutional principles that make America exceptional and the beacon of light to the world.

THE DEGRADATION OF EDUCATION IN BLACK COMMUNITIES

When he was attorney general, Bill Barr said, our public education system is "a racist system, maintained by the Democratic Party and the Teachers Union."

The goal of the far left, from the inception of this nation, has been to overthrow the chief principle of limited government (that is of, for and by the people) and to limit individual freedoms. To achieve this goal, the left understood that it would take decades to shift America's cultural identity. To do this, they knew they had to control the levers of education.

The school system that inner-city children are forced into is a tragedy. The Democratic Party-run, failing public schools are setting Black Americans up for failure from the beginning. An investigation done by Project Baltimore analyzed the 2017 state testing data. It found one-third of high schools in Baltimore had no students proficient in math. None. This is not just the case in Baltimore. Investigations across country find this tragic pattern to be normal in most inner-city schools. A California study found that only 20 percent of Black students in the entire state are proficient in math and only 33 percent were proficient in English. This is evidence that no institution is driving racial inequality, as effectively as public schools.

These numbers shock my conscience. When I found out about this, I couldn't believe what I was hearing. How can a country as powerful as the Unites States allow this to happen? Even in the third-world nation I come from, Zimbabwe, this is not the case. In Zimbabwe, if you're not proficient at your grade level in math or English, you're forced to repeat the grade before they let you just slide through. To avoid the embarrassment of having to repeat a grade, many parents put their children through "holiday school." It is common, and relatively inexpensive, to have a private tutor help to get their children up to speed.

How is this real injustice—graduating the country's youth when they can't read on a third-grade level—allowed to continue? Why is this absent from the national conversation about so called social justice and so-called equity? Why are students not being taught the basic skills they need to be productive members of society?

When you consider the average amount that the taxpayer pays per student in these failing schools, the numbers become even more disturbing. The national average being spent per pupil, is a whopping twelve thousand dollars per year. In Democratic run states, like New York and Connecticut, the expenditure is nearly nineteen thousand dollars per year, per student.

My children attend a private Christian school. Their school offers an excellent classical education, demands academic excellence, and provides a safe environment. The cost of this superior education, which produces critical thinkers and problem solvers, is less than the average per-student cost for public schools.

Good education is the best path for breaking out of a low-income stratum. It worked for both myself and my husband.

Democrats, in collusion with the teachers' unions, vigorously fight to keep inner-city children trapped in the failing schools. They are, in effect, sentenced by district, based on their zip code. My friend Lisa, an advocate for school choice, calls it "zip code jail." Students are only allowed to attend the public school in their school district. Poor parents, typically Black or Hispanic, are forced to enroll their children in underperforming schools. This is the case, even if there are better schools nearby or just blocks away from their homes. This rigid districting system gives underperforming schools a monopoly. This monopoly model for failing schools ensures underperforming schools continue to operate. Sadly, the worse the schools perform, the more money they demand and are given.

School choice is a program that is championed by the Trump administration as the solution to this social injustice. School choice gives parents of poor families the choice to take their children to better performing public schools and charter schools, and in some cases, they can use government vouchers to pay for private school.

This model creates competition. To compete for students, the underperforming schools would be forced to improve their standards. If unable to improve their standards, then under performing schools would be forced to shut down.

Creating a competitive environment among schools would raise the standard of education in the inner-city across the nation. With several options for school, parents would have the freedom to choose the best school that fits the needs of their child.

This all sounds great, right? Who would oppose giving parents options for schooling their children? Democrats continue to fight school choice tooth and nail. Isn't it amazing that the party of the "right to choose," meaning the disposal of your unborn child in the third trimester of pregnancy, considers the desire of parents to choose a school for their children as zealotry?

Democrats often tell Blacks that racism is the most pressing issue we face in America. Yet in the last fifty years, few things have hurt Black Americans more than the inner-city public school systems. For decades, the teacher's unions and Democrats have openly supported the zip code jails that have resulted in resegregated public schools.

Rich and middle-class Americans already have school choice. They can afford to live in nice areas. Many relocate from blue cities to surrounding suburbs, specifically for a better school districts. In most places, the better the school system, the higher the prices of homes. This makes it difficult for kids whose parents can't afford to live in more affluent areas to escape the zip code jails.

The teachers' unions and their allies in the Democratic Party actively oppose charter schools, religious schools, and even home schooling. This is despite overwhelming data, showing the effectiveness of these good alternatives. One reason is that the teachers' unions can't extort teachers in the latter school systems to pay union dues. This is the reason why, for decades, the teachers' unions has worked to have charter and private schools shut down.

Poll after poll demonstrates that minority families are in support of school choice. Unfortunately, Democrats get away with ignoring this issue. Every election cycle, instead of addressing why the education is failing Black youth, the Democratic Party convinces Black people that the number one issue they face is racist White cops. Even though, in 2019, a grand total of nine unarmed Black men were killed by police officers. The real tragedy is that millions of Black kids are not getting a proper education. As a result, their chances for success are greatly diminished. Their slice of the American pie continues to get gobbled up by the teachers' unions. Their chance at the American Dream is the only thing being systematically murdered.

Over the past sixty years, the miseducation of American children has had catastrophic consequences. Not only for the individual, but also collectively on American culture and societal norms. If the left's conveyor belt keeps rolling on, then these consequences will determine whether or not America, "the land of the free," will survive with its founding ideals intact.

RECLAIMING EDUCATION IS THE KEY

It starts with a reformation of the education system. At the end of her conveyor-belt illustration, my friend Lisa said the most powerful thing Lucy and Ethel could have done in the scene was simply flip the switch and turn off the conveyor belt.

TAKE BACK EDUCATION WITH SCHOOL CHOICE

I believe taking back education is the foundational key to changing the progressive left's direction of this country. Education is also a key issue that Conservatives and Republicans can leverage to court Hispanic and Black voters. According to polls, 70 percent of both Hispanic and Black voters are in favor of school choice. Black and Hispanic Americans want school choice but are currently stuck with having to put their children in failing inner-city schools run by Democrats and teacher's union financiers.

Speaking at the "Transition to Greatness" roundtable, President Trump called upon Congress to enact school choice, hailing it as the great "civil rights issue of our time."

"We are renewing our call on Congress to finally enact school choice now, school choice is a big deal, because access to education is the civil rights issue our time," the President said. "I've heard that for the last, I would say year, it really is, it's the civil rights issue of our time."

President Trump gets it. Because he's not beholden to special interests, who line the pockets of politicians, President Trump mostly operates on his gut instinct of what he thinks is the right thing to do. Of course, giving parents the option to take their children to a better school is the right thing to do. But for Democrats, pleasing the teachers' unions that line their pockets is what matters most to them.

The teachers' union bosses are raking in billions of dollars per year off the public school system that guarantees customers, even though they fail to satisfy the customer. According to a news report by journalist Perry Chiaramonte, the average teacher makes forty-four thousand per year, while the average union boss makes five hundred thousand per year, on the low end. As teachers face pay freezes and layoffs, the teachers' unions saw their pay increase 20 percent in 2012 alone, according to his investigation.

The public school system operates like a monopoly that has no incentive to satisfy their customers. The government has created conditions, where the competition to this monopoly have been wiped out, forcing consumers to buy only from one company. At this company, incompetent employees (teachers) are not allowed to be fired under any circumstances (tenure).

The big teachers' unions are a key reason for the failure of the American public's education. The public school system is now essentially designed to serve the teachers' unions. They are a special interest group, protecting the status quo and a system that rewards mediocrity and incompetence. The union contract structures individual teacher's jobs in ways that offers them no incentives for excellence in the classroom and instead rewards failure.

Former public school teacher Rebecca Friedrichs was the lead plaintiff in Friedrichs vs. California Teachers' Association. She tells us how the national unions have gotten so corrupt: "[Teachers unions] are riding on their great past when they did some wonderful things, but they literally have become what they used to fight." She adds, "The schools cannot and will not improve until reformers confront the grave consequences of the power that teachers' unions wield over an industry that that is set up to be monopolistic."

Reform is needed in the way the contracts are written. Teachers that are producing results (producing students who are proficient) must be rewarded. While those teachers who are failing at educating kids should be let go. But reform in the contracts is not enough. The unions' influence on the elected officials who regulate the education industry must be addressed too. Until then, any reform, whether smaller classes, more money for the schools, or high national standards, will not yield the desired result.

As schools continue to fail children, more demands for more money in the schools are made to remedy the situation. But the extra money being poured into these schools has benefited the unions, and to a smaller extent the teachers, but has not improved student performance.

According to the National Assessment of Education Progress data, average SAT scores for public school students have declined, dropout rates in urban school systems have increased, and American students scored at or near the bottom, in comparisons with the other industrialized nations.

Meaningful education reform that addresses these core issues is highly unlikely anytime soon, given the deep pockets of these unions and the influence they have on Democratic politicians in Washington. They give millions to these politicians, who in return, ensure the monopoly of the public-school system is maintained. According to the Center of Response Politics, from 2004 to 2016, teachers' unions donations to Democrats grew from 4.3 million dollars to more than thirty-two million—an all-time high.

Teachers at private schools and charter schools, are not required to pay union dues. This means less money for the teachers' union. To ensure an evergreen flow of billions of dollars each year into their coffers, teachers' unions must ensure all competition to the public-school system is stomped out. The Democratic Party has been ready, willing, and able, to make that happen for them, to the detriment of the American student.

The 250-billion-dollar public education industry is essentially a publicly protected monopoly. Creating competition would force public schools to improve their standards, to attract "customers," aka students.

END THE PUBLIC SCHOOL SYSTEM

In doing research on the public school system for this book, I have been shocked at what I have learned. Where I grew up in Zimbabwe, I never experienced the American public school system, so it has all been surprising to me. Two of the most surprising things I have learned are the amount money spent on education and the fact that despite all this money being spent on education, millions of young Americans (mostly minority Americans) are being graduated without being proficient, after six hours a day and thirteen years of learning.

To me, this is the biggest miscarriage of justice in America. Former Attorney General Bill Barr was right when he said, "If there is systematic racism in America, look no further than our public school system." This is a system maintained by the Democratic Party that, according to Barr, specializes in "keeping inner-city kids in failing schools, instead of putting the resources in the hands of the parents to choose the schools to send their kids to." He goes on to say, "That's empowering kids. That's giving them a future."

Besides not being proficient in basic subjects, an equal injustice is what they are being taught to believe about themselves, their fellow citizens, and the revised history of this great nation.

After studying just how far the rabbit hole goes in the public school system, I'm almost convinced it's beyond redemption. Instead of engaging in the bare knuckles political fight it would take to reform this corrupt system, it makes more sense to create a parallel and competing privately run system.

The school choice program, as championed by President Trump, is a great start. President Trump has urged Congress to pass his Education Freedom Scholarships (EFS) proposal.

A Washington Times article described this program:

Under the President's EFS proposal, taxpayers could make voluntary contributions to scholarship-granting organizations, which would be identified and approved by states, and these organizations would give out scholarships to students that could be used for a wide variety of educational options. Taxpayers making contributions would receive a non-refundable dollar-for-dollar tax credit.

EFS would not be a top-down federal program but would allow states to decide whether to participate and how to select eligible students, education providers and allowable education expenses. Among the expanded educational opportunities that states could approve include advanced, remedial and elective courses; career-technical-education certifications; private and home education; special education services and therapies; tutoring; and summer and after school education.

During a round table discussion on school choice with the President, an African-American man, Walter Blanks, described a similar program as having changed his life.

The scholarship allowed Walter, who struggled in public school, to escape an environment that resulted in prison or worse for so many of his peers. "This is life or death," he told the President. "The only difference is that I had a way out" through the scholarship program.

Republicans have introduced bills in Congress that would fund students directly and not the schools. The bills would restrict the federal government from any influence over school curriculum, practices, and admission policies, which would be a big win. One bill, the SCHOOL Act, introduced by Senator Rand Paul, would allow federal education funds to follow a child to the public school, private school, or home school program of their parent's choice.

If passed, these laws would dismantle the stronghold the public school system has on the children of America. This would create the competition needed to force the public school system to reform itself or go out of business. With an annual average of twelve to twenty-two thousand dollars being spent per pupil on a substandard education, this money would be better spent on private and charter schools.

If passed, school choice bills, would not only forbid discrimination against private and home education providers, but it would allow federal funds to be used for and by religious educators.

EVERY CHURCH *MUST* START A CHRISTIAN SCHOOL

My friend Lisa has dedicated her life to working on education reform. Her goal is to render public schools irrelevant and she has the blueprint to do it. This may seem like a lofty goal, but it can be done. Conservatives are for the private sector on every other issue, but they bristle at the thought of the government no longer educating our kids. Why?

This blueprint will come alongside current school choice programs. Following the Supreme Court's ruling that struck down a state ban on taxpayer funding for religious schools, known as the *Espinoza* decision, there is a real prospect that the church, and by extension conservatives, can take back the reins of education.

I'm a strong advocate for a Christian education. I put my money where my mouth is, and I cannot imagine it any other way. The idea of walking my children to the bus stop to be picked up by the big yellow bus every morning and entrusting their little malleable minds to progressive teachers and educators doesn't sit well with me. Every effort made to instill conservative Christian values in my home, would be undermined as soon as they got to school. Yet, the majority of Christians and conservatives do just that. Many, because they may not have a choice.

I was listening to conservative radio show host Chris Plante when an angry listener called in about his daughter. He told Chris that he had spent tens of thousands of dollars on his daughter's college education. Every month, when he had to pay tuition, he said his blood pressure would go up. He went on to say that what he got out it was "a thirty-five-year-old, pot smoking, Bernie supporter living in his basement with a liberal arts degree she cannot do anything with!" I thought, "Wow!" Unfortunately, this is the same for a vast number of Christians and conservative parents.

In the late nineteenth century, the majority of America's population was Protestant Christian. Public schools were effectively Protestant schools. Prayer and Bible reading were standard. Because Catholics didn't want their children educated by Protestants, they began to build their own schools. Protestants were fine with Catholics having their own schools, but they balked at any taxpayer funds being designated for them. So they began a campaign to ensure that no tax funds were designated for religious education.

Because Protestants already controlled the public school system, they went along with laws that prohibited thirty-seven state's tax dollars from being used for religious education. These provisions became known as the Blaine Amendment, in honor of Representative James Blaine, who championed the cause.

After secularists gained control of the public schools, following a series of Supreme Court decisions in the 1960s, this backfired on Protestant Christians. The Blaine Amendment was intended to create a religious monopoly in favor of Protestants, but it ended up serving the interests of the secularists.

In a lengthy article, Joseph Backholm, senior fellow at the Family Research Council, details all of this and the need for churches to take on the role of educating. He laments at the fact that "Protestants, unlike Catholics, continue to take their children to public schools, even as schools became more secular." Today, of the 70 percent of Americans that claim to be Christian, 90 percent of them send their children to public schools. The results, as I detailed in earlier chapters, are devastating. The only way to change course is to take a radically different approach.

The *Espinoza* decision is a door that has opened for Christians and conservatives to reclaim territory on the education mountain. In reclaiming influence on education, many of the other spheres of influence will begin to come into alignment. For example, a strong educational foundation, that also teaches the value of personal responsibility, will create a harvest of people who understand that the choices they make in life are what ultimately determines their destiny. Instead of a generation of people who are crippled by victimhood, believing they can't succeed, because of their skin color.

Will the church and political Conservatives partner to take advantage of this opportunity to take back the schools? It's going to require hard work. It's going to mean taking on the teachers' unions, who are working overtime to ensure school choice programs are not adopted.

While the Supreme Court has made it legal for religious schools to take advantage of school choice programs, it's the state legislatures that determine whether school choice programs exist. This means the church must partner with conservative activists (called to the political sphere of influence) and work with state-elected officials to create or expand school choice programs.

To save the next generation from falling away to the far-left world view they are being inducted into, we have to create the infrastructure. Parents must be given the choice, and children must be given the opportunity, to be formed in a different environment.

There are approximately ninety thousand public schools in America. On the other hand, there are over three hundred thousand churches in America. Creating Christian schools at already existing churches is a brilliant and practical way to invest in children's futures. It is also the way to plant seeds of evangelism, fulfilling the Great Commission to make disciples. Church buildings sit empty ninety percent of the time. Why not use those building to facilitate education during the week?

Parents who are not religious or of another faith are open to taking their child to a Christian school with an excellent academic track record. They come for the academics, but they also get a Christian conservative world view.

An abundance of Christian schools that are funded through tax credits and school choice programs, will be a great option for the 90 percent of Christians who have their kids in public schools. Christians will now have an affordable opportunity to put their children in a Christian school that teaches their children values that are consistent with the values they are taught at home.

As a result of years of education, that is antithetical to Christianity, too many Christian children are falling away from the faith. One thing has become abundantly clear, we can't offset thirty hours a week in a secular school with ninety minutes of Sunday school. According to Joseph Backholm, "The Church must end the habit of outsourcing the education of kids and once again become the greatest influence in the lives of our children. Our ambition needs to be much bigger than church attendance; we need to create an environment where Jesus can capture their hearts and become the object of their affections."

Granted, this is ambitious. It will take strategic planning and execution to have churches begin to start schools. With seven hundred billion dollars being poured into failing public schools annually, some of those funds can be redirected to churches for education. This would provide a financial incentive for many churches, as well as the evangelical incentive of discipling the next generation.

"The journey of a thousand miles starts with the one step," said Backholm. "A church can start with the small step of starting a kindergarten and expanding from there. Within a decade or sooner you have a real school." We must start thinking generationally and we must start to make bold moves.

CHAPTER 11

BLACK ECONOMIC EMPOWERMENT VS POLITICAL POWER

In this book, I have detailed how the left was able to infiltrate every sphere of society and gain influence and control over the levers of cultural power. The plan has been to remove the godly and moral foundations of America and replace it with a socialist/ Marxian world view.

In recent years, the progressive left's main weapon of choice to gain power has been race. Posing as the friend and benefactor of Black people and minorities, they managed to position themselves as moral and virtuous. Because they now control more than 90 percent of the media, they have been successful at cementing this image of their false virtue in the hearts and minds of millions of Americans. They have been equally as successful in portraying their political opponents as racist and evil.

Operating under the guise of helping the Black people, the left implemented policies that have ultimately harmed the Black community. These policies were not designed to empower Black people but to keep many poor and economically dependent on government. Their policies led to the systematic dismantling of the Black family structure by removing the Black father from the home. This resulted in the fracturing of Black society, which has ultimately led to higher levels of poverty, crime, violence, school dropouts, drug use, and more.

Through mass media propaganda, the left has managed to scapegoat America as being a White supremacist nation for their own failed policies. For fifty years, they've made a compelling case to Black America that the reason for any failures that have occurred in their society is because they are victims of an oppressive system that is designed to keep them from ever amounting to anything. This message has been engrained in the hearts and minds of millions of Black Americans and has unfortunately become a self-fulfilling prophecy for some.

Every election cycle, Black Americans have yielded their electoral power almost exclusively to the Democratic Party. In exchange they have gotten nothing of value. Instead, mental shackles have been placed on the minds of many, stifling their progress and potential.

Success begins in your mind. The foundation of success is a positive mind-set. Nothing is achieved without a belief that it can be done. So when Black people are told by their parents, teachers and culture that they're victims of oppression and therefore can't get ahead, that mind-set begins to manifest that reality. I know I certainly would not be where I am in life today if I didn't have a mother who instilled in me a can-do attitude and the work ethic to match.

BLACK POLITICAL POWER

In studying Black American history during the period after slavery and before the 1960s, I see many cultural similarities they shared with the culture I was raised in in Africa. It's a culture that cultivates personal responsibility and self-determination (Black Americans who are successful today exhibit these same qualities).

This has led me to believe that one of the solutions for Black America is to rediscover who they were before the 1960s and post slavery. This is a period in Black American history that has been largely memory holed because it does not fit the modern-day cultural narrative of what it means to be Black in America.

From post-slavery 1890 to the 1940s, Black Americans were focused primarily on developing their human capital. They were focused on educating themselves, becoming more literate, learning valuable skills, and empowering themselves economically. During this time, blacks knew they could not depend on government, so they set about doing what it took to empower themselves, and it was working. Wealth and income gaps between blacks and Whites were rapidly shrinking during this period. Home ownership among blacks was rising rapidly, and crime in Black communities was very low.

The shift came in the 1960s, following the voting rights act of 1965, when blacks shifted their focus from acquiring economic empowerment to wanting political empowerment. The Black leaders of that day sought to elect more Black people into positions of political power. Their thinking was that the more Black people they had in government, the better the lives of Black people would become.

Black Americans were highly successful in their quest to acquire more political clout. According to author Jason Riley, Blacks holding a political office went from fifteen hundred in the 1970s to over ten thousand by 2010. This includes Black mayors, Black congressmen, Black governors, Black police chiefs, and of course, the first Black president. Sadly, more Black people in positions of political power has not resulted in the betterment of Blacks economically or by any other metric. Poor Blacks have progressively become poorer despite an increase in Black political power.

The idea that electing more people that share the same skin color as you is going to result in your greater economic advancement, is a misplaced idea. I come from a country where the entire government shared my skin color and race but did nothing to facilitate the economic advancement of the people that elected them.

Black Americans have been sold the idea that, for Black people to advance, they must elect people that share their skin color. I'm here to tell you it doesn't work that way, and eight years of the first Black President has more than demonstrated that. It's the policies the person represents that matter, not whether or not they're Black.

President Obama's policies hardly benefitted the Black community, and we saw a decline in just about every metric within the Black community over the course of his term. Prominent Black American author and talk show host Tavis Smiley lamented the lack of economic progress amongst Black Americans since Obama entered office. He said, "Sadly — and it pains me to say this — over the last decade, Black folk, in the era of Obama, have lost ground in every major economic category." He goes on to say Black America "got caught up in the symbolism of the Obama presidency," which resulted in hesitance to critique his failed policies.

By contrast, in under three and a half years of President Trump (who is falsely portrayed as a racist by the left's media), Black people have seen great economic advancement. Georgia State Representative Vernon Jones (a Black American) said President Trump "has done more for the Black community in under four years than Joe Biden has done in more than forty."

What Democratic Party candidate for president Joe Biden has to show for his forty-seven years in politics, is the 1994 Crime Bill that mass incarcerated thousands of Black men since its enactment. Joe Biden sponsored this bill and helped draft it. He was very proud of this bill. In a 1993 speech, Joe Biden warned of "predators on our streets," who were beyond redemption, "beyond the pale," and he said they must be removed from society because the justice system did not know how to rehabilitate them.

Joe Biden belongs to a party that has spent decades telling Black people that they can never make it in America because they do not possess White privilege. The Democratic Party has an army of rich Black people (mostly athletes and entertainers) on cable TV, radio shows, and on social media, that spend a lot of their time telling poor Black people that they can never be rich because of racism. Think about that—rich Black people telling Black people they can never be rich because of racism. The irony is mind-blowing.

These are wealthy Black people that are successful because they worked hard, persevered, and took advantage of their God given talents and the American opportunity. Yet they conceal their formula for success from other Black people and instead parrot a victim narrative that does not promote the values that got them where *they* are.

BLACK ECONOMIC EMPOWERMENT

For the most part, chasing political clout has not worked for Black Americans, so maybe it's time to go back to seeking personal development and economic empowerment. Big government is not the answer. Black people were thriving in many areas during that period between slavery and the 1950s, because big government was not involved in their lives.

Rather than focusing on electing more Black people to higher office, based on their skin color, not the policies they represent, it is time to focus on electing more people (regardless of their race) who represent policies that will economically empower all people. Black people must support policies that create an environment where people are free to thrive. That means policies that make it easy to own and run a business, lower taxes, and less regulations. They need policies that make it hard for American companies to move their factories abroad so that good high paying manufacturing jobs are created here in America.

In 2016, President Trump challenged Black America to vote for him. He was the first Republican candidate in decades to court the Black American vote to the horror of Democrats (who need at least 92 percent of the Black vote to win elections).

Then candidate Trump said, "You're living in poverty; your schools are no good; you have no jobs; 58 percent of your youth is unemployed—what do you have to lose?" Indeed, the Black community had nothing lose. Though a small percentage of the Black community took him up on this offer in 2016, President Trump, nonetheless, was able to accomplish more for Black Americans in one term than the Democrats have in the last fifty.

Some of President Trump's accomplishments for the Black community include "opportunity zones," which direct and incentivize private investment in Black communities, creating jobs and development of distressed communities.

President Trump lowered taxes and increased access to capital, which led to a 400 percent increase in Black business ownership in his first year. Plus, we have seen the lowest Black unemployment rate in American history. His pro-America trade deals have allowed many of the high paying manufacturing jobs to come back. Many of those blue color jobs are filled by Black Americans, who are now moving into the middle class.

President Trump's, passage of the First Step Act, represents the most consequential reform on criminal justice in decades. He reversed Joe Biden's Crime Bill, which led to decades of mass Black incarceration. Prison reform is reducing the Black incarceration rates. It also gives thousands of non-violent offenders a new lease on life with reforms that focus on reintegrating these former inmates into society.

President Trump also signed an executive order to permanently fund Historically Black Colleges and Universities (HBCUs) with ten billion dollars of annual funding.

In September of 2020, President Trump announced his Platinum Plan for Black America, which he plans on rolling out in his second term if elected. This is his plan to bring economic empowerment back to the Black community. Here are three of the policies he seeks to enact.

1. Five hundred billion dollars in business capital designated to ignite Black businesses
2. Make the office of Minority Business Development Agency permanent
3. Second Step Act, that will build on the achievements of the First Step Act

President Trump projects that his plan will create five hundred thousand new Black businesses, which will bring prosperity and self-sufficiency to many in the Black community.

Like him or not, President Trump has the "hand-up" not "handout" blueprint on what it's going to take to narrow the economic disparities between Black and White Americans. Ultimately it is going to take Black America doing their part in pursing that economic empowerment.

CONSERVATIVE'S OUTREACH TO BLACK AMERICANS

As conservatives and Christians, we have an opportunity to take President Trump's lead on reaching out to our brothers and sisters in Black and minority communities. We have an opportunity to impact these communities in a positive way that brings healing to the nation and turns the tide away from progressivism. After all, Black Americans (historically) and Hispanic Americans are conservative in their values. Yet, they overwhelmingly vote for the Democratic Party which is moving further and further to the left away from traditional values.

The disconnect has been a lack of outreach as well as poor messaging on the part of conservatives. We have not been able to effectively communicate who we are and what we stand for. For decades, the media has defined us as racists, homophobes, sexists, and bigots. President Trump has not been an exception to these smears by the media, however, he has been able to penetrate through media noise to Black and minority voters. His common-sense approach to problems that plague minority communities and clear messaging has penetrated the hearts and minds of many.

Given a chance in his second term, President Trump's school choice program, coupled with his economic empowerment Platinum Plan, would give Black people educational choice and a higher prospect of prosperity. Following President Trump's economic empowerment policies instead of Democratic dependency policies, Black Americans can participate in the American dream for a bright future.

A large percentage of the Black American community is waking up to the reality of the Democratic failures. Many are no longer willing to blindly vote Democrat. As we near the November election, independent poll numbers show that President Trump is set to double his support among Black and Latino voters, when compared to his 2016 support. This is despite a 24/7 Democratic media propaganda machine that smeares the president as a racist White supremacist.

This is very promising. Whatever the outcome of this election, we are starting to see cracks in the Democrat's monopoly and grip on the Black vote. We are seeing early signs of a coming exodus from the Democratic Party. Some in the Black community are choosing to walk away from the perpetual state of victimhood, dependency, bitterness, and anger sold by the Democratic Party. Many are realizing they can choose to walk in love and forgiveness and take advantage of the opportunities around them.

AMERICA'S CHOICE: MARXISM VS. LIBERTY

I'm writing this book about choices at a time when the American people have collectively come face to face with what will be our most important choice that will ultimately determine whether the American Republic survives and lives on with its foundational principles intact.

America was founded on these top five principles:

- Faith in God as the Creator and moral governor of the universe (our rights come from God not Government).
- Belief in the Bible as the source of ultimate truth.
- Human nature flawed by sin cannot be trusted with ultimate power (limited government, separation of powers).
- Morality is essential for a stable and prosperous nation.
- Government exists to protect life, liberty, and private property.

These five principles are what made America great, exceptional, and the most prosperous nation on Earth.

For a hundred years, these foundational principles have been under a slow but relentless assault. The values that make this country great have been systematically eroded over time, taking

America further away from its God-given destiny as the beacon of liberty, hope, and opportunity. An astounding acceleration of this erosion has taken place in the last ten years.

The 2020 election will be a flash point that could go one of two ways for America:

1. This election could very well be the left's final and irreparable blow to America as we have known it.
2. Or, with the reelection of President Trump, this could be the year America begins to reverse course from the century long slide to the far left.

When the dust settles, for better or worse, things are never going back to the way they used to be. In this final chapter, I'll discuss where I see the country going depending on the how things turn out in this pivotal election. This is not an ordinary election. America is at a fork in the road and the path we choose will determine whether this year marks the end of America as we know it or America lives on preserving its founding principles.

THE END OF AMERICA AS WE KNOW IT?

With the globalist forces he has behind him, if Joe Biden is inaugurated, America as we know it will be no more. It has been the left's goal to fundamentally change America. In 2008, Obama vowed, "We are five days away from fundamentally transforming the United States of America." Joe Biden echoed Barack Obama's 2008 promise to fundamentally transform America during an interview with the press in mid-April of 2020, stating that Coronavirus was "an incredible opportunity to fundamentally transform the nation."

By contrast, to be a conservative is to conserve as much as possible, the founding values, principles, and culture of America. I, like many conservatives, don't want to see America fundamentally transformed. We want to see essence and the ideals of America preserved.

Conservatives recognize that this year's election could be our last opportunity to conserve the American way. We must not be foolish and naïve in thinking that if we miss it, we're just going to wait four more years and hope another conservative is elected. If you're like me, and pay attention to politics, you know the left is on a crusade to take full control over the reins of power, not for an election cycle but permanently. This is not hyperbole on my part; this is what they have been effectively announcing all year.

Democrats are now openly calling for an end of the electoral college, adding Puerto Rico and Washington DC as states (to add four more leftist senators), an end to the filibuster rule, and packing the Supreme Court with more liberal justices (to counteract the new six-to-three conservative–liberal split). I recognize this rhetoric for what it is—an attempt at a permanent power grab.

Ending the electoral college would ensure that smaller, less populous states would be powerless to elect a president. Popular vote presidential elections would be decided by two to three high population Democratic controlled states, like New York and California.

The United States, as founded by the Constitution, was not formed as a democracy. America is a constitutional republic. The left works overtime to undermine the virtues and the brilliance of the electoral college. They try to sell Americans a bad bill of goods, saying that majoritarianism is a profound moral good. The founders of the country believed that a diffuse democracy, like the one the electoral college provides, weakened the ability of politicians to rely on emotional appeals of fear or otherwise to take power.

Now that Democrats believe they have the numbers, they are pushing for a system, where politicians who promise the most-free stuff, to the largest number of people, win. In so doing, Democrats are no longer hiding their attempts to overthrow the foundational ideas of American governance.

After solidifying their power in Congress by removing the filibuster, stacking the Court, and abolishing the electoral college, the next thing Democrats plan on doing is opening the flood gates of illegal immigration.

Millions of illegal migrants, promised free healthcare and housing (courtesy of the generous taxpayers), will flood into the country. It would be naïve to think Democratic politicians are motivated by compassion. It's not compassion, I can assure you. They're motivated by self-interest. Mass unbridled immigration will all but guarantee the Democrats a large evergreen voter base that would ensure that no opposition party would ever challenge their dominance.

Just as they have done over the last fifty years with the many in the Black community, Democrats will keep their new voter base poor, dependent on government, and voting Democrat.

In my opinion, this new voter base will be weaponized as a political machine that will overturn every constitutional freedom in America. Every far-left policy they have been wanting to enact will become a reality. They'll raise taxes across the board, regulate small businesses out of existence, restrict gun rights, defund the police, and institute government control of every aspect of our lives. If you think I'm exaggerating, just look to California, which is a microcosm of what the rest of the country can look forward to if the left is able to get full control.

Under the weight of so-called progressive policies, California now has the highest rates of poverty and homelessness in the country. There has been a mass exodus of the middle class out of California to conservative run states, like Texas and Arizona. Californians are fleeing high taxation, high regulations, crime, a strain on resources like schools due to mass, unbridled immigration and government intrusion on every aspect of life.

In signing a "unity pact" with Socialist Senator Bernie Sanders, Joe Biden has signed on to progressive and socialist policies. President Trump called Joe Biden a Trojan Horse for the firebrand radical left in his party, which, in my opinion, is an accurate assertion.

We have witnessed the Democratic party move further to the left, embracing very radical far-left ideologies, political correctness, cancel culture, and extreme identity politics. This has triggered millions of Americans to leave the party. Former gay Democrat and New Yorker turned conservative Brandon Straka started a movement called the #WalkAway Movement following his viral video that got over a hundred million views. In the video, he shares why after voting Democrat all his life, he was walking away. The walkaway movement has since drawn hundreds of thousands of former Democrats to share their "walk away" testimonies on social media.

Prominent Democrats, like Black civil right lawyer Leo Terrell, have recently joined the movement, saying (just like Ronald Reagan did), "I didn't leave the Democrat Party, the Democrat Party left me." Former NFL player and former avid President Obama supporter Jack Brewer has also walked away from the Democratic Party. Now he vigorously supports President Trump. He cites his reason as, "the Party's extreme departure from Christian values." These are just a couple of examples, of many prominent Democrats, including elected officials, who have

walked away from the party due to it's departure from mainstream American values.

OR THE REBIRTH OF AMERICA?

For the last four decades, politicians in Washington (both parties) made millions of dollars selling influence to globalist powers and foreign governments at the expense of the American people. They enacted policies that resulted in millions of jobs being shipped to China and elsewhere. A massive wealth transfer from the United States to China and other foreign counties ensued, leaving America with an ever-shrinking middle class. As politicians got richer in Washington, the American people got poorer.

In 2016, Donald Trump showed up on the scene, riding in on a populist wave of a growing number of Americans who had become increasingly disgruntled at the establishment elites in Washington DC, who no longer served the interests of the American people but rather the interests of foreign countries and entities that lined their pockets.

Trump promised to reverse the one-sided trade deals signed by his predecessors and restore America's jobs and wealth. He promised to put the interests of the American people first. He could not be bought by special interest groups because he made his wealth in business. So, he kept his promises, and in doing so, he disrupted the Washington establishment's status quo. He shined a light on the massive corruption that was going on at the expense of the working men and women of America. For four years, they have tried relentlessly to run him out of town.

It remains to be seen what direction the country goes. This election is pivotal because it is not about electing a person or a personality. It is not even about electing one of two parties. It is about electing one of two futures for America. Will America make the right choice?

The reelection of President Trump would represent conserving America as founded. The preservation of the values and principles that made America exceptional. The restoration of the power and wealth of the people in what historians will look back on as the second American Renaissance. A revolt against an encroaching globalist Communism and the end of the American ideals.

At a glance, the odds seem to be against America. America is fighting the seemingly all-powerful globalist establishment machine, that is now firing on all cylinders, to stop the populist rebellion against them by preventing a Trump second term, "by any means necessary!" The mainstream media is essentially a 24-hour, seven-days-a-week Biden campaign ad that runs on all the major networks. All pretense of objectivity has gone out of the window, as 94 percent of the coverage of President Trump is hostile, regardless of any good deed he does.

Silicon Valley tech giants Google, Facebook, and Twitter have launched an all-out war against the free flow of information by censoring any information critical of Joe Biden and the Democratic Party. Twitter even went so far as to censor entire news organizations, like the *New York Post*, whose account was suspended for weeks following its exposé on the damning content of Hunter Biden's infamous laptop.

I'm experiencing the censorship firsthand, as I find myself suspended from my Twitter account for days for the crime of posting my opinions on Biden that are being labeled as "misinformation." My Facebook and Instagram accounts are being throttled and shadow banned as the statistics on my posts now reflect a drastic drop in audience reach.

Who made the tech elites in Silicon Valley the arbiters of what's true or false? Millions of Americans are now being censored online and thrown into digital gulags where they can't be seen or heard. The internet is the twenty-first century public square, and if we're not free to speak there, we've lost our First Amendment constitutional right to free speech.

It's frightening to watch America go down this path. This is precisely the kind of authoritarianism we're up against as a country. The basic freedoms we've enjoyed for so long are at stake.

The good news is the rising tide of the populism has only gotten larger since 2016. Because the movement has gotten so much stronger, the establishment elites in the media, Washington, DC, and Silicon Valley have been forced to be heavy handed in their desperate quest to stop the populist surge. That has only served to awaken even more people to their sinister ways. I would be confident of a big victory for President Trump, if I didn't see the inevitable problems that will ensue as a result of the unprecedented mail-in balloting scheme being proposed.

If the reelection of President Trump becomes a reality, we face a renewed hope, of not only stopping the advances of the left, but also reversing the tide. This is not a task for President Trump, but his presence in the White House for a second term would make the journey easier for "We the People" to take our positions at the gates of influence.

Conservatives, patriots, and Christians must occupy the cultural spheres of influence that have been abdicated to the left for so long. We must take back the territory we lost in the spheres of education, media, politics, arts and entertainment, family, and business.

Our nation's core values are what makes America great and the most exceptional, prosperous, innovative, and free nation in the history of this planet. The cyclical norm in world history has been that a small group of elites, monarchs, chiefs, kings, or queens ruling over many.

Although the American Revolution was derived from Western civilization, shaped by Judeo-Christian culture and the political liberties inherited from Great Britain, the founding of America was unique and revolutionary. It was a rebellion, not in the sense of overthrowing the institutions of society or rulers, but in placing political authority in the hands of the common person, the individual, "We the people."

It's a revolutionary idea that the only source of the legitimate powers of government is the consent of the governed. This ideal of American government and society, is the foundation of what makes America truly special.

This is what gives me a sense of urgency and the reason why I have become politically engaged in the the journey to save America. I truly love this country. We must not let this nation fall to Marxism. Like many hardworking immigrants, I was drawn to this beacon of opportunity. Opportunity that is not common in most nations.

As an immigrant, I came to America with nothing, but I was able to lift myself out of poverty and ascend to greatness. In 2020, my life is a testament to the fact that the American dream is alive and well. I want to see this nation survive and thrive as founded. I want my children to grow up in the America that provided me the liberty, safety, and prosperity that I now enjoy.

FINAL THOUGHTS

Individually, the choices we make are ultimately what determines what circumstances we find ourselves in. Yes, life throws curve balls at us that are beyond our control. We can't control what circumstances we're born into. But we can control how we respond to the cards life has dealt us. Privilege comes in many forms, but ultimately, the privilege we can control, comes from the choices we make daily, some big, some small. As believers, we must choose to be the light in the spheres of influence that God has called each of us to.

Collectively as Americans we face a choice. The decisions we make and actions we take, will determine whether or not we keep our American privilege and freedom. Freedom is not free. It has been bought and paid for by the blood of the many brave men and women, of every race, color and creed, who fought before us. Even though elections are pivotal, turning this nation back to its founding ideals is neither something that can be accomplished in one election cycle nor by one man. The yoke is too heavy of a burden for one man to carry alone. As the saying goes, 'many hands make light work.' Each and every one of must play our small parts. To turn the tide, we must choose to engage with the political mountain. We can no longer standby and passively live our lives in the fruitful valleys of this nation.

As the United States, we must choose to reject the left's divisive tactics and reunite under the American ideals that make us great. The ideals this free nation was founded upon must be conserved and perpetually fought for.

What will America choose? What will you choose to do?

APPENDIX

INTRODUCTION AND CHAPTER 1

1. Jason Whitlock, "Black Pride Religion Ordained by White Liberals Taking Black People and America Straight to Hell" https://www.outkick.com/whitlock-black-pride-religion-ordained-by-white-liberals-taking-black-people-and-america-straight-to-hell/

2. David Satter,"100 Years of Communism-and 100 Million Dead" https://www.wsj.com/articles/100-years-of-communismand-100-million-dead-1510011810

3. White Privilege. Merriam-Webster's Unabridged Dictionary, s.v. "White Privilege" accessed September 19, 2020, https://www.merriam-webster.com/dictionary/white%20privilege

4. Noam Shpancer, "Unearned Advantage: What to Make of 'Privilege,'" *Psychology Today*, https://www.psychologytoday.com/gb/blog/insight-therapy/202007/unearned-advantage-what-make-privilege

5. "Privilege, Discrimination and Racial Disparities in the Criminal Justice System," *ADL*, https://www.adl.org/education/educator-resources/lesson-plans/privilege-discrimination-and-racial-disparities-in-the

6. Peggy McIntosh, "White Privilege: Unpacking the Invisible Knapsack," *Racial Equality Tools*, https://www.racialequitytools.org/resourcefiles/mcintosh.pdf

7. Herbert London, "The Close-Minded Campus? The stifling of ideas in American Universities," Discussion Panel, https://www.youtube.com/watch?v=aAhrNoiSuQE

8. ADL White Privilege https://www.adl.org/education/resources/tools-and-strategies/kyle-korver-privilege-and-racism

9. Peggy McIntosh, https://en.wikipedia.org/wiki/Peggy_McIntosh

10. Peggy McIntosh, "White Privilege and Male Privilege: A Personal Account of Coming to See Correspondences Through Work in Women's Studies," *WCW Online*, accessed July 9, 2020, https://www.wcwonline.org/images/pdf/White_Privilege_and_Male_Privilege_Personal_Account-Peggy_McIntosh.pdf

11. Jordan Peterson, "Postmodernism: Definition and Critique," accessed September 19, 2020, https://www.jordanbpeterson.com/philosophy/postmodernism-definition-and-critique-with-a-few-comments-on-its-relationship-with-marxism/

12. Jordan Peterson, "Identity Politics and the Marxist Lie of White Privilege," https://www.youtube.com/watch?v=PfH8IG7Awk0

13. Hannah Sparks, "Oprah Labeled a 'Fraud' for Calling Out White Privilege Since She's So Rich," *New York Post*, https://nypost.com/2020/08/05/oprah-criticized-for-calling-out-white-privilege-since-shes-rich/

14. Jeff Myers, "Marxism in America? Yes," *Summit*, https://www.summit.org/resources/articles/marxism-america-yes/

15. American enterprise Institute. Panel discussion. "The Close-Minded Campus? The Stifling of Ideas in American Universities," https://www.youtube.com/watch?v=aAhrNoiSuQE

16. *Analytical Economist*, "White Privilege Debunked in One Chart," https://thefederalistpapers.org/us/white-privilege-debunked-in-one-chart

17. Peter D., "Privilege/Class/Social Inequalities Explained in a 100 Race," https://www.youtube.com/watch?v=4K5fbQ1-zps

18. United States Census Bureau, "Median Income by Race," https://www.census.gov/topics/income-poverty/income.html

CHAPTER 2

1. Ben Carson, *Gifted Hands: The Ben Carson Story*, (Michigan: Zondervan, December 1996

2. Candace Owens, *Blackout*, (New York: Simon and Schuster, 2020, 129

3. Biography, "Robert Mugabe Biography," https://www.biography.com/political-figure/robert-mugabe

CHAPTER 3

1. Britannica, "Robert Mugabe, President of Zimbabwe," https://www.britannica.com/biography/Robert-Mugabe

2. South African History Online, "Robert Gabriel Mugabe," https://www.sahistory.org.za/people/robert-gabriel-mugabe

3. Ron Haskins Brookings, "Three Simple Rules Poor Teens Should Follow to Join the Middle Class," https://www.brookings.edu/opinions/three-simple-rules-poor-teens-should-follow-to-join-the-middle-class/

CHAPTER 4

1. A. W. R. Hawkins, "The Democrat Party: Keeping Black down Since 1964," https://humanevents.com/2010/07/14/the-democratic-party-keeping-blacks-down-since-1964/

2. TFPP Writer, *Federalist Papers*, "Here's What LBJ's Great Society has Really Done for Black Americans," accessed September 22, 2020, https://thefederalistpapers.org/us/heres-what-lbjs-great-society-has-really-done-for-black-americans

3. *Smithsonian*, "Everett Dirksen: Forgotten Civil Rights Champion," https://npg.si.edu/blog/everett-dirksen-forgotten-civil-rights-champion

4. Library of Congress, "The Civil Rights Act of 1964: A Long Struggle for Freedom," https://www.loc.gov/exhibits/civil-rights-act/civil-rights-act-of-1964.html

5. Jon Miltimore, "Did LBJ Say 'I'll Have Those N*ggers Voting Democratic for 200 Years," https://www.intellectualtakeout.org/blog/did-lbj-say-ill-have-those-nggers-voting-democratic-200-years/

6. Thomas Sowell Quote, "The Black Family Liberalism a De Facto Attack on Blacks," https://blog.libertasbella.com/thomas-sowell-quotes/

7. Fred Siegel, "The Forgotten Failures of the Great Society," https://www.nationalreview.com/magazine/2020/01/27/the-forgotten-failures-of-the-great-society/

8. Lindsey M. Burke, "The Not So Great Society" https://www.heritage.org/the-not-so-great-society

9. Brock Griffin. "The Extent of the Fatherless", https://fathers.com/statistics-and-research/the-extent-of-fatherlessness/

10. United States Census Bureau, "Two Extremes of Fatherhood," https://www.census.gov/library/stories/2019/11/the-two-extremes-of-fatherhood.html

11. US Department of Health and Human Services, "ASEP Issue Brief: Information on Poverty and Income Statistics," accessed on September 12, 2020, http://aspe.hhs.gov/hsp/12/PovertyAndIncomeEst/ib.shtml

12. Daniel Patrick. Moynihan Report, *The Negro Family: The Case for National Action*, (New York: Cosimo Reports)

13. Jason Riley, *False Black Power*, (New York: Templeton Press, First edition, 2017) 38.

14. Hoover Institution, "Jason Riley Interview," https://www.youtube.com/watch?v=bi2hqL5KkHc

15. Jason Riley, *Please Stop Helping Us*, (New York: Encounter Books, 2016).

16. Thomas Stowell,. *Black Redneck and White Liberals*, (New York: Encounter Books, 2009,) Audio: https://www.youtube.com/watch?v=LdRBCFaslbo

17. Candace Owens, *Black Out: Blackout on Culture*, (New York: Simon and Schuster, 2020, 29).

18. Valerie Richardson, "Smithsonian African American Museum Removes 'Whiteness' Chart as Racist," accessed on September 22, 2020, https://www.washingtontimes.com/news/2020/jul/17/smithsonian-african-american-museum-remove-whitene/

CHAPTER 5

1. Paul Kengor, *The American Thinker*, "Progressives and Communists: Out of the Closet— Together," https://www.americanthinker.com/articles/2010/10/progressives_and_commu- nists_ou_1.html

2. Cleon Skousen, *The Naked Communist*, (Scotts Valley, CA, Create Space Publishing 9th edition July 1961)

3. John Eidson, *Canada Free Press Blog*, "The Communist Plan to Overthrow America from Within," https://canadafreepress.com/article/the-communist-plan-to-overthrow-america-from-within

4. "The Naked Communist—Sixty Years Later," https://historicaltruthproject.com/2020/06/22/ the-naked-communist-sixty-years-later/

5. *Merriam-Webster's Dictionary*, "marxism," https://www.merriam-webster.com/ dictionary/Marxism

6. Seraphim Hanisch, "Jordan Peterson on Why Marxism Is Attractive Despite history's record https:// theduran.com/jordan-peterson-on-why-marxism-is-attractive-despite-historys-record-video/

7. Jordan Peterson, "Postmodernism: Definition and Critique," https://www.jordanbpeterson. com/philosophy/postmodernism-definition-and-critique-with-a-few-comments-on-its-rela- tionship-with-marxism/

8. "Mass Killings under Communist Regimes," https://en.wikipedia.org/wiki/ Mass_killings_under_communist_regimes

9. Hellen Pluckrose, "How French 'Intellectuals' Ruined the West: Post Modernism and Its Impact," https://areomagazine.com/2017/03/27/ how-french-intellectuals-ruined-the-west-postmodernism-and-its-impact-explained/

10. *Encyclopedia Britannica*, "Postmodernism," https://www.britannica.com/topic/ postmodernism-philosophy

11. Doug Mainwaring, "TV Networks to Air Commercial Depicting Menstruating Men and Boys," https://www.lifesitenews.com/pulse/ tv-networks-to-air-commercial-depicting-menstruating-men-and-boys

12. Emily James, "I've Gone Back to Being a Child: Husband and Father of Seven, 52 Leaves his Wife and Kids to Live as Transgender Six-Year-Old Girl," https://www.dailymail.co.uk/ femail/article-3356084/I-ve-gone-child-Husband-father-seven-52-leaves-wife-kids-live- transgender-SIX-YEAR-OLD-girl-named-Stefonknee.html

13. Ben Shapiro, "Why Has the Western Civilization Been So Successful," Prager U Video, https://www.youtube.com/watch?v=RVD0xik-_FM

CHAPTER 6

1. *Britannica*, "Critical Race Theory," https://www.britannica.com/topic/critical-race-theory

2. Carol Swain, "Critical Race Theory Is Rooted in Cultural Marxism," https://americaoutloud. com/critical-race-theory-is-rooted-in-cultural-marxism/

3. Brant Bosserman, "Marxism, Postmodernism, and Critical Race Theory," https://www.theaquilareport.com/marxism-postmodernism-and-critical-race-theory/

4. *Tucker Calrson Tonight*, "Critical Race Theory Has Infiltrated the Federal Government," Christopher Rufo Interview on Fox News, https://www.youtube.com/watch?v=rBXRdWflV7M

5. James Lindsay, "Eight Big Reasons CRT Is Terrible for Dealing with Racism," https://newdiscourses.com/2020/06/reasons-critical-race-theory-terrible-dealing-racism/ https://founders.org/2020/02/03/critical-race-theory-intersectionality-and-the-gospel/

6. Mark Moore, "Trump Expands Ban on Critical Race Theory to Federal Contractors," https://nypost.com/2020/09/23/trump-expands-ban-on-critical-race-theory-to-federal-contractors/

7. Tamar Lapin, "Merriam-Webster Will Update 'Racism' Definition after Request," https://nypost.com/2020/06/09/merriam-webster-will-update-definition-of-racism-after-a-request/

8. Coleman Hughes, "Review of Ibram Kendi's Book, *How to Be an Anti-Racist* How to Be An Anti-Intellectual," https://www.city-journal.org/how-to-be-an-antiracist

9. Tyler O'Neil, "The Real Problem with 'Anti Racism,'" https://pjmedia.com/columns/tyler-o-neil/2020/09/08/the-real-problem-with-anti-racism-n907714

10. Tom Ascol, "Critical Race Theory, Intersectionality, and the Gospel," accessed on September 30, 2020, https://founders.org/2020/02/03/critical-race-theory-intersectionality-and-the-gospel/

11. *What Would You Say*, Youtube, "Is Critical Race Theory Biblical?" https://www.youtube.com/watch?v=DAABuCC96tI

12. *Oxford Dictionary*, "Racism," https://www.oxfordlearnersdictionaries.com/us/definition/english/racism

13. Thomas Sowell, *Black Redneck and White Liberals Slavery*, (New York: Encounter Books, Audio Book, 2009,) https://www.youtube.com/watch?v=LdRBCFaslbo

14. Rachel Morgan, PhD and Barbara A Oudekerk, *Criminal Victimization 2018*, "Interracial Violence," https://www.bjs.gov/content/pub/pdf/cv18.pdf

15. Jason Riley, *Please Stop Helping Us*, (New York, Encounter Books; Reprint Edition, 2016.)

16. Staff, "Cops Seek Teens Who Allegedly Set Fire to 13-Year-Old Student," *Crimesider*, https://www.cbsnews.com/news/cops-seek-teens-who-allegedly-set-fire-to-13-year-old-student/

CHAPTER 7

1. Larry Elder Quote from Twitter Feed, https://twitter.com/larryelder

2. BLM Website, https://blacklivesmatter.com/about/

3. Ryan Bomberger, *Radiance Foundation*, https://townhall.com/columnists/ryanbomberger/2020/06/05/top-10-reasons-i-reject-the-blm-n2570105

4. Matin Luther King Jr. "I Have a Dream," Speech https://www.mtholyoke.edu/acad/intrel/speech/dream.htm#:~:text=In%20the%20process%20of%20gaining,plane%20of%20dignity%20and%20discipline.

5. David Horowitz, "Black Lives Are a Pretext," https://www.frontpagemag.com/fpm/2020/06/black-lives-are-pretext-david-horowitz/

6. Angelo Fichera, "Donations to Black Lives Matter Don't Go to the DNC," https://www.fact-check.org/2020/06/donations-to-black-lives-matter-group-dont-go-to-dnc/

7. Craig Luther, "BLM Movement: An Existential Threat to America" https://www.front-pagemag.com/fpm/2020/06/blm-movement-existential-threat-america-dr-craig-luther/

8. The Okra Project, "To Black Trans People," https://www.theokraproject.com/sponsors-donors-1

9. FBI Crime Stats, https://ucr.fbi.gov/crime-in-the-u.s/2018/crime-in-the-u.s.-2018/tables/table-43

10. Joseph Wulfsohn, "CNN's Chris Cuomo Blasted for Suggesting Protesters Don't Have to Be Peaceful," https://www.foxnews.com/media/cnns-chris-cuomo-blasted-for-suggesting-protesters-dont-have-to-be-peaceful

11. Rebecca Klar, "Kenosha Police Say Most of Arrests During the Protests Were from out of Town," https://thehill.com/homenews/state-watch/514417-kenosha-police-say-most-arrest-ed-during-protests-were-from-out-of-town

12. *Western Journal*, "Police Shooting and Interaction," https://www.westernjournal.com/stats-systemic-police-racism-myth/

13. Centers for Disease Control and Prevention, "Leading Cause of Death—Male-Non-Hispanic Black—United States," https://www.cdc.gov/healthequity/lcod/men/2017/nonhispan-ic-black/index.htm

14. Ryan Saavedra, "Mac Donald: Statistics Do Not Support The Claim Of 'Systemic Police Racism'" *The Daily Wire,* accessed August 8, 2020, https://www.dailywire.com/news/mac-donald-statistics-do-not-support-the-claim-of-systemic-police-racism

15. KSTU-TV, "Salt Lake Cop Cleared in Shooting of Unarmed White," accessed on August 15, 2020, https://wreg.com/news/salt-lake-cop-cleared-in-shooting-of-unarmed-white-man/

16. Elisha Fieldstadt, "75-Year-Old White Man Thrown to the Ground by Police," accessed August 22, 2020, https://www.nbcnews.com/news/us-news/75-year-old-man-shoved-ground-buffalo-police-suffered-brain-n1230421

17. Thomas Sowell, quote on racism, https://www.azquotes.com/quote/880482

18. Moreno Edward, "Minneapolis Parks and Recreation Board Follows School Board in Ending Relationship with Police Department," *The Hill,* https://thehill.com/homenews/state-watch/501243-minneapolis-parks-and-recreation-board-follows-school-board-in-ending

19. James Rainey, "Growing the LAPD Was Gospel at City Hall. George Floyd Changed That," *Los Angeles Times,* https://www.latimes.com/california/story/2020-06-05/eric-garcetti-lapd-budget-cuts-10000-officers-protests

20. Sara Dorn, "Shootings Soar 205 Percent after NYPD Disbands Anti-Crime Unit," *New York Post*, https://nypost.com/2020/07/04/shootings-soar-205-percent-after-nypd-disbands-anti-crime-unit/

21. Ashley Southall and Michael Gold, "1-Year-Old Is Shot and Killed at Brooklyn Cookout," *New York Times*, https://www.nytimes.com/2020/07/13/nyregion/Davell-Gardner-brooklyn-shooting.html

22. Brittany Kriegstien, "'When Is It Going to End?': Grandmother Grieves, Rages Over Baby in Stroller Killed by Gunfire at Brooklyn Cookout," *Daily News*, https://www.nydailynews.com/new-york/nyc-crime/ny-baby-fatally-shot-stroller-brooklyn-park-cookout-20200713-hso2f-b63r5bsjebq7ltp2ki5gu-story.html

23. Lydia Saad, "Black Americans Want Police to Retain Local Presence," *Gallup News*, https://news.gallup.com/poll/316571/black-americans-police-retain-local-presence.aspx

24. Robert Johnson, BET Founder in Fox News Interview, "Black Americans Laugh at White People," https://yournews.com/2020/06/28/1700775/pew-analysis-shows-only-1-in-6-blm-protesters-are/

25. People Magazine: Chrissy Tiegen Donates $200L to Help Bail Out Protestors Across the US," accessed August 22, 2020, https://people.com/tv/chrissy-teigen-donates-200k-to-help-bail-out-protesters-george-floyd-death/

26. Rebecca Klar, "Kenosha Police Say Most Arrested During Protest Were from out of Town," accessed August 22, 2020 https://thehill.com/homenews/state-watch/514417-kenosha-police-say-most-arrested-during-protests-were-from-out-of-town

27. Katrina Schollenberger, "Fighting Back: Who is Ariel Atkins and what did she say about the Black Lives Matter protest in Chicago?" accessed August 23, 2020 https://www.thesun.co.uk/news/12376076/ariel-atkins-black-lives-matter-chicago-looting/

28. Martha MacCallum, "New York BLM Leader Hawk Newsome Defends Looters, Compares American to Terrorists," *Daily Mail,* accessed August 23, 2020 https://www.dailymail.co.uk/news/article-8643543/amp/New-York-BLM-leader-Hawk-Newsome-defends-looters-compares-America-terrorists.html

29. Sister Toldjah. "Fed Up Minneapolis Woman Gives Interview That Every Riot Apologist in the Mainstream Media Should Watch" *Red State,* accessed August 23, 2020, https://redstate.com/sister-toldjah/2020/05/30/fed-up-minneapolis-woman-gives-interview-that-every-riot-apologist-in-the-mainstream-media-should-watch-n138604

30. Jeff Mordock, "Chicago Records Most Violent Weekend this Year with More than 100 Shootings and 14 Deaths," *Washington Times*, https://www.washingtontimes.com/news/2020/jun/22/chicago-records-most-violent-weekend-year-more-100/

31. Tara C. Jatlaoui, MD, "Abortion Surveillance United States 2014," accessed on August 25, 2020 https://www.cdc.gov/mmwr/volumes/66/ss/ss6624a1.htm

32. Alveda King Quote on abortion during a meeting of Priests for Life https://margaretsanger.blogspot.com/2007/08/niece-of-martin-luther-king-jr-abortion.html

33. Kristen Hawkins, "Remove Statues of Margaret Sanger, Planned Parenthood Founder Tied to Eugenics and Racism," *USA Today*, https://www.usatoday.com/story/opinion/2020/07/23/racism-eugenics-margaret-sanger-deserves-no-honors-column/5480192002/

34. Margaret Sanger commenting on the "Negro Project" in a letter to Gamble, December 10, 1939.

35. Kevin Vance, "Sec. Clinton Stands by Her Praise of Eugenicist Margaret Sanger," *Washington Examiner*, August 26, 2020, https://www.washingtonexaminer.com/weekly-standard/sec-clinton-stands-by-her-praise-of-eugenicist-margaret-sanger

36. Ken Blackwell, "President Obama to Abortionists: Thank You Planned Parenthood, God Bless You," accessed on September 2, 2020, https://www.charismanews.com/opinion/50755-president-obama-to-abortionists-thank-you-planned-parenthood-god-bless-you

37. Arina Grossu, "Margaret Sanger, Racist Eugenicist Extraordinaire," accessed on September 2, 2020, https://www.washingtontimes.com/news/2014/may/5/grossu-margaret-sanger-eugenicist/

38. E. Coleman, "Margaret Sanger Journal," *The Birth Control Review 1917*, September 5, 2020, https://sangerpapers.wordpress.com/tag/birth-control-review/

39. Full Text: President Trump quote at pro-life rally, https://www.lifesitenews.com/news/full-text-trumps-2020-march-for-life-speech

40. Andrew McCarthy, "Understanding Black on Black Murders," *National Review*, https://www.nationalreview.com/corner/understating-black-on-black-murders/

CHAPTER 8

1. Mark Moore, "Rep. Ilhan Omar Calls to Dismantle 'Rotten Minneapolis Police Department," *New York Post*, https://nypost.com/2020/06/08/rep-omar-dismantle-rotten-minneapolis-police-department/

2. Edward Moreno, "Minneapolis Park and Recreation Board Follows School Board in Ending Relationship with Police Department," *The Hill*, https://thehill.com/homenews/state-watch/501243-minneapolis-parks-and-recreation-board-follows-school-board-in-ending

3. Rusty Wies, "Abolish Police and Prisons Goes Mainstream at the DNC," *Political Insider*, https://thepoliticalinsider.com/abolishing-police-and-prisons-goes-mainstream-at-the-dnc/

4. Jack Brewster, "LA Mayor Slashes LAPD Budget as Calls to Defund Police Slowly Pick up Steam," *Forbes*, https://www.forbes.com/sites/jackbrewster/2020/06/04/la-mayor-slashes-lapd-budget-as-calls-to-defund-police-slowly-pick-up-steam/?sh=207ef40d1ba3

5. Sara Dorn, "Shootings Soar 205% after NYPD Disbands Anti-Crime Unit," *New York Post*, https://nypost.com/2020/07/04/shootings-soar-205-percent-after-nypd-disbands-anti-crime-unit/

6. Ashley Southhall, "1-Year-Old Is Shot and Killed at Brooklyn Cookout," *New York Times*, https://www.nytimes.com/2020/07/13/nyregion/Davell-Gardner-brooklyn-shooting.html

7. Tristan Justice, "Gallup: 81 Percent of Black Americans Want Police Protection, Some Want More," *The Federalist*, https://thefederalist.com/2020/08/06/gallup-81-percent-of-black-americans-want-police-protection-some-want-more/

8. Leah Barkoukis, "BET Founder Explains Why African Americans Are Laughing at White People," *The Town Hall*, https://townhall.com/tipsheet/leahbarkoukis/2020/06/26/bet-founder-blacks-mocking-whites-n2571390

9. Victoria Bekiempis, "The New Racial Makeup of US Police Dept.," accessed July 23, 2020, https://www.newsweek.com/racial-makeup-police-departments-331130

10. Maurice Richards, "The Myth of an Epidemic of Racist Police Shootings Is Wrong and Dangerous," accessed July 23, 2020, https://dailycaller.com/2019/11/24/epidemic-racist-police-shootings/

11. Julie Tate, "Fatal Force: 999 People Were Shot and Killed by Police in 2019," accessed July 22, 2020, https://www.washingtonpost.com/graphics/2019/national/police-shootings-2019/

12. Ryan Saavedra, "Mac Donald: Statistics Do Not Support the 'Claim of Systemic Police Racism,'" accessed July 22, 2020, https://www.dailywire.com/news/mac-donald-statistics-do-not-support-the-claim-of-systemic-police-racism

13. Andres Jauregui, "Officer's Fatal Shooting of Unarmed Man Dylan Taylor Was Justified," *Huffington Post*, https://www.huffpost.com/entry/dillon-taylor-shooting-justified_n_5912976

14. Sarah Taddeo, "75-Year-Old Man Pushed to Ground by Buffalo Police 'Come Front a Peace Tradition,'" *USA Today*, https://www.usatoday.com/story/news/nation/2020/06/05/martin-gugino-pushed-ground-buffalo-police-known-peaceful-man/3160820001/

15. Candace Owens. *Blackout: How Black America Can Make Its Second Escape from the Democrat Plantation.* (New York: Simon and Schuster, 2020), 221.

16. Thomas Sowell quote. https://www.azquotes.com/author/13901-Thomas_Sowell/tag/racism

CHAPTER 9

1. Dian Rufino, "The Johnson Amendment and the Silencing of the Church," *Beaufort County Now*, https://www.beaufortcountynow.com/post/17899

2. Bill Johnson, *Invading Babylon.* (Shippensburg, PA: Destiny Image Publishers July 1st 2013), 18.

3. Allison McCalman, "The History of Christian Education in America," *The Classroom*, https://www.theclassroom.com/the-history-of-christian-education-in-america-12080826.html

4. *Wikipedia*, "Counterculture of the 1960s," https://en.wikipedia.org/wiki/Counterculture_of_the_1960s

5. Dr. Lance Wallnua. *Invading Babylon: How Do We Take Over the World*, (Shippensburg: Destiny Image Publishers, 2013,) 102.

6. Austin Cline, "Engel v. Vitale Abolished Public School Prayer," *ThoughtCo*, Aug. 29, 2020, thoughtco.com/engel-v-vitale-1962-249649.

7. Penny Starr, "Education Expert: Removing Bible, Prayer from Public Schools has Caused Decline," *CNSNews*, https://www.cnsnews.com/news/article/penny-starr/education-expert-removing-bible-prayer-public-schools-has-caused-decline

8. William Jeynes, "Putting Bible and Prayer Back in Public School," speech at the Heritage Foundation in Washington, DC. Aug. 13, 2014, https://www.frc.org/get.cfm?i=ev14f04

9. George Washington, Farewell Address 1796. US Embassy and Consulate in the Republic of Korea, https://kr.usembassy.gov/education-culture/infopedia-usa/living-documents-american-history-democracy/george-washington-farewell-address-1796/#:~:text=And%20let%20us%20with%20caution,in%20exclusion%20of%20religious%20principle

10. David Miller, "President Trump Signs 'Johnson Amendment' Executive Order Limiting Treasury's Action against Religious Organizations Engaged in Political Campaign Activities," *National Review,* accessed on July 9, 2020, https://www.natlawreview.com/article/president-trump-signs-johnson-amendment-executive-order-limiting-treasury-s-actions

11. Caleb Parke, "New York Celebrates Legalizing Abortion until Birth as Catholic Bishops Question Cuomo's Faith," *Fox News*, https://www.foxnews.com/politics/new-york-celebrates-legalizing-abortion-until-birth-as-catholic-bishops-question-cuomos-faith

12. Abraham Hamilton, "BLM's Doctrine of Demons," *SkywatchTV* Podcast 9/10/20 https://www.skywatchtv.com/videos/five-in-ten-9-10-20-abraham-hamilton-iii-blms-doctrines-of-demons/ Abraham Hamilton, "Marxist Lies Matter," American Family Radio https://afr.net/podcasts/the-hamilton-minute/2020/july/marxist-lies-matter/

13. Damian Thomas, "Is Black Lives Matter a Religion for Woke White People?:" *Spectator*, https://spectator.us/black-lives-matter-religion-woke-white-people/

14. Publisher. "Wokeness Is the New Religion and Christians Are Converting En Masse," *Pulpit and Pen*, https://pulpitandpen.org/2020/06/09/wokeness-is-a-new-religion-and-christians-are-converting-en-masse/

15. "Our Demands," Black Lives Seattle, https://blacklivesseattle.org/our-demands/

16. Clinton Yates, "BLM Groups Release Demands, *The Undefeated*, https://theundefeated.com/whhw/black-lives-matter-groups-release-demands/

17. Ryan Foley, "BLM Leaders Practice 'Witchcraft' and Summon Dead Spirits, Black Activist Claims," *Christian Post*, https://www.christianpost.com/news/blm-leaders-practice-witchcraft-and-summon-dead-spirits-black-activist-warns.html

18. Abraham Hamilton, "BLM Connection to Witchcraft," YouTube video, https://www.christianpost.com/news/blm-leaders-practice-witchcraft-and-summon-dead-spirits-black-activist-warns.html

19. Darrel Harrison, "Black Lives Matter?" *Just Thinking Podcast*, Episode 102

20. Darrel Harrison, "Church of BLM," *Just Thinking Podcase*, Episode 103

21. John Calvin, *Institutes of the Christian Religion*, Published 1536

22. Lance Wallnauw, "Three Keys to Changing Culture," Facebook post, https://lancewallnau.com/category/culture-transformation/

23. David Chilton, Paradise Restored: A Biblical Theology of Dominion (Waterbury Center,VT: Dominion Press, 1984).32.

CHAPTER 10

1. Matthew Spalding, PhD, "Why Is America Exceptional?" *Free Republic*, http://www.freere-public.com/focus/f-news/2608846/posts

2. Lydia Saad, "The US Remained Center Right, Ideologically, in 2019," *Gallup Poll*.

3. Ebony Bowden, AOC Says its Likely Biden Will Move Farther to the Left Once in Office," *New York Post*, https://nypost.com/2020/09/17/aoc-says-its-likely-biden-will-move-farther-left-once-in-office/

4. Joel Pollack, "9 Radical Ideas in the Biden-Sanders Unity Platform," *Brietbart*, https://www.breitbart.com/podcast/2020/07/09/9-radical-ideas-in-the-biden-sanders-unity-platform/

5. Backet Adams, "Biden Disavows Green New Deal Co-Sponsored by Kamala Harris," *Washington Examiner*, https://www.washingtonexaminer.com/opinion/joe-biden-disavows-new-green-deal-co-sponsored-by-kamala-harris

6. Kate Sullivan, "Larry Kudlow: The Green New Deal Will Literally Destroy the Economy," *CNN*, https://www.cnn.com/2019/02/28/politics/larry-kudlow-green-new-deal-destroy-economy/index.html

7. Jon Levine, "Confessions of a Voter Fraud: I Was a Master at Fixing Mail-in Ballots," *New York Post*, https://nypost.com/2020/08/29/political-insider-explains-voter-fraud-with-mail-in-ballots/

8. Mark Hemmingway, "28 Million Mail-in Ballots Went Missing in the Last 4 Elections," *Real Clear Politics*, https://www.realclearpolitics.com/articles/2020/04/24/28_million_mail-in_ballots_went_missing_in_last_four_elections_143033.html

9. Kevin Jessip, Speech at the the Return Rally, in Washington, DC, https://www.youtube.com/watch?v=RPriyeJ_Pl4

10. Ellison Barber. "New York, District Result Delayed More than a Month after Mail-in Vote," *MSN*, https://www.msn.com/en-us/news/politics/new-york-district-results-delayed-more-than-a-month-after-mail-in-voting/vi-BB17ocoJ

11. Dr. Susan Berry, "Poll: Democrats Divided on School Choice along Racial, Ethnic Lines" *Breitbart*, https://www.breitbart.com/politics/2019/08/20/poll-democrats-divided-on-school-choice-along-racial-ethnic-lines/

12. Justin Vallejo, "Trump Says 'School Choice' Is the Civil Rights Issue of All Time in This Country,'" *MSN*, https://www.msn.com/en-gb/news/world/trump-says-school-choice-is-the-civil-rights-issue-of-all-time-in-this-country/ar-BB15zWcV

13. Perry Chiarrmonte, "Average Teacher Makes $44 Thousand Dollars while the Average Union Boss Makes $500 Thousand," *Fox News*, accessed October 3, 2020, https://www.foxnews.com/us/average-teacher-makes-44g-while-their-top-union-bosses-pull-in-nearly-500g

14. Julia Machester, "Former Public School Teacher Says Unions Are Becoming What They Used to Fight," *The Hill*, https://thehill.com/hilltv/rising/446344-former-public-school-teachers-says-unions-are-becoming-what-they-used-to-fight

15. Sol Stern, "How Teachers Unions Handcuff Schools," *City Journal*, https://www.city-journal.org/html/how-teachers%E2%80%99-unions-handcuff-schools-12102.html

16. Jonathan Rothwell, "The Decline Productivity of Education," *Brookings*, https://www.brookings.edu/blog/social-mobility-memos/2016/12/23/the-declining-productivity-of-education/

17. "Teachers Unions Top Contributors," *Open Secrets*, https://www.opensecrets.org/industries/indus.php?ind=L1300

18. Ian Hanchett, "Barr: Our Public Education System Is a Racist System Maintained by the Democratic Party and the Teachers Unions," *Breitbart*, https://www.breitbart.com/clips/2020/08/13/barr-our-public-education-system-is-a-racist-system-maintained-by-the-democratic-party-and-the-teachers-union/

19. Lance Lzumi, "Trump's School Choice Program Will Help Kids and Is Smart Politics," *Washington Times*, https://www.washingtontimes.com/news/2020/jan/4/trumps-school-choice-plan-will-help-kids-and-is-sm/

20. Joshau Nelson, "Student Touts Trump's Push for School Choice: Everything Changed For Me After Receiving Private Scholarship," *Fox News*, https://www.foxnews.com/media/trump-fighting-school-choice-walter-blanks

21. Deborah Simmons, "Rand Paul's SCHOOL Act Is Spot On," *Washington Times*, https://www.washingtontimes.com/news/2020/aug/17/rand-pauls-school-act-is-spot-on/

22. Ilya Somin, Supreme Court Strikes Down Montana Blaine Amendment Barring State Aid to Religious Schools," *Reason*, https://reason.com/2020/06/30/supreme-court-strikes-down-montana-blaine-amendment-barring-state-aid-to-religious-schools/

23. Joseph Backholm, "Why Every Church Must Start a Christian School," *FRC*, https://www.frc.org/issuebrief/why-every-church-should-start-a-christian-school

CHAPTER 11 AND CONCLUSION

1. Ashely Lutz, "These 6 Corporations Control 90% of the Media in America," *Business Insider*, https://www.businessinsider.com/these-6-corporations-control-90-of-the-media-in-america-2012-6?op=1

2. Jason Riley, *False Black Power* (New York: Templeton Press, 2017,) 11.

3. Rahel Gebreyes, "Tavis Smiley: Black Americans Have 'Lost Ground' under Obama," *Huffington Post*, https://www.huffpost.com/entry/tavis-smiley-obama-black-wealth_n_569820dbe4b0ce496423f053

4. Tyler O'Neil, "Trump Did More for Black Americans in 4 Years than Biden Did In 40, Says Vernon Jones" *PJ Media* https://pjmedia.com/election/tyler-o-neil/2020/09/23/trump-did-more-for-black-americans-in-4-years-than-biden-did-in-40-vernon-jones-says-n960693

5. The Scoop, "Flashback: Joe Biden's Infamous And Racist 1993 Crime Bill Speech," https://www.thegatewaypundit.com/2020/10/flashback-joe-bidens-infamous-racist-1993-crime-bill-speech-video/

6. Andrew Kaczynski, "Biden in 1993 Speech Pushing Crime Bill Warned of 'Predators On Our Street' Who Were Beyond the Pale," *CNN*, accessed October 4, 2020, https://www.cnn.com/2019/03/07/politics/biden-1993-speech-predators/index.html

7. Anders Hagstrom, "What Do You Have to Lose? Trump Tells Black Americans to Give Up on the Left," *Daily Caller*, https://dailycaller.com/2020/09/25/trump-black-americans-blm-biden-democrats/

8. Jack Davis, "Trump to Roll Out $500 Billion Platinum Plan for Black America," *Western Journal*, https://www.westernjournal.com/trump-rolls-500-billion-platinum-plan-black-americans/

9. Eddie Hyatt, "5 Founding Principles That Made America Great," *Charisma News*, https://www.charismanews.com/politics/opinion/71951-5-founding-principles-that-made-america-great

10. Victor Davis Hanson, "Obama: Transforming America," *Real Clear Politics*, https://www.realclearpolitics.com/articles/2013/10/01/obama_transforming_america_120170.html

11. Allan Smith, "Some Dems Want to End the Electoral College," *NBC News*, https://www.nbcnews.com/politics/donald-trump/some-dems-want-end-electoral-college-trump-says-it-s-n985256

12. Jordan Carney, "Bitter Fight Over Barret Fuels Calls to End the Filibuster and Expand," *The Hill*, https://thehill.com/homenews/senate/523050-bitter-confirmation-fight-fuels-calls-to-nix-filibuster-expand-court

13. Clay Jenkinson, "The Electoral College Explain: Its History And Tension Of Democracy," *Governing*, https: https://www.governing.com/context/The-Electoral-College-Explained-Its-History-and-the-Tensions-of-Democracy.html

14. Joe Pollak, "9 Radical Ideas in Biden-Sanders Unity Platform," *Breitbart*, accessed October 15, 2020, https://www.breitbart.com/podcast/2020/07/09/9-radical-ideas-in-the-biden-sanders-unity-platform/

15. Christie Lee McNally, "Big Tech's Censorship of Conservative Uses Is Alive and Well," *The Hill*, https://thehill.com/opinion/cybersecurity/397047-big-techs-censorship-of-conservative-users-is-alive-and-well

CPSIA information can be obtained
at www.ICGtesting.com
Printed in the USA
BVHW041305260321
603517BV00013B/85/J